photographing
the Adirondacks

Where to Find Perfect Shots and How to Take Them

Carl Heilman II

THE COUNTRYMAN PRESS
WOODSTOCK, VERMONT

Maps by Paul Woodward, © The Countryman Press
Book design and composition by S. E. Livingston

Photographing the Adirondacks
978-1-58157-187-5

Published by The Countryman Press,
P.O. Box 748, Woodstock, VT 05091

Distributed by W. W. Norton & Company, Inc.,
500 Fifth Avenue, New York, NY 10110

Printed in the United States of America

10 9 8 7 6 5 4 3 2 1

*Title Page: Great horned owl at the Adirondack
Wildlife Refuge*

The High Peaks from Algonquin Peak, second-highest mountain in the state

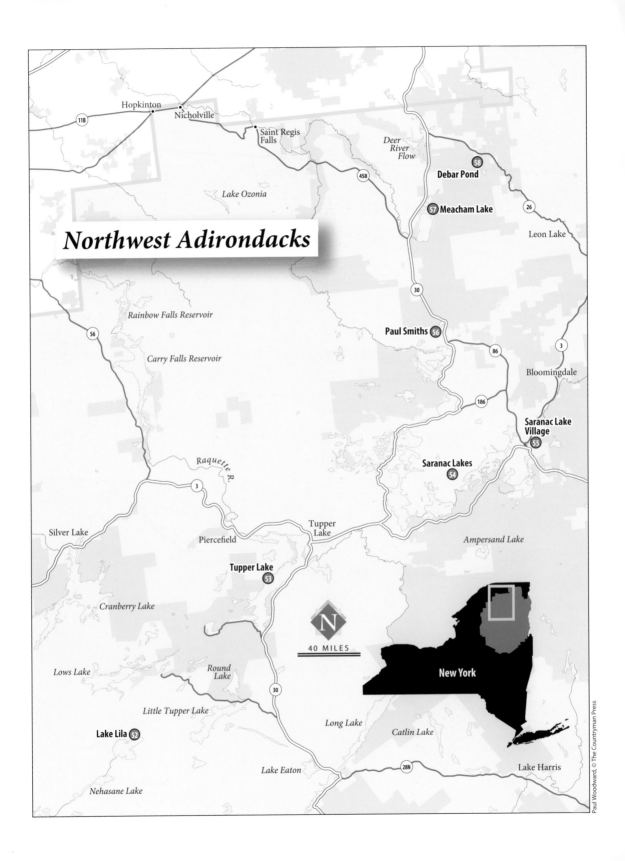

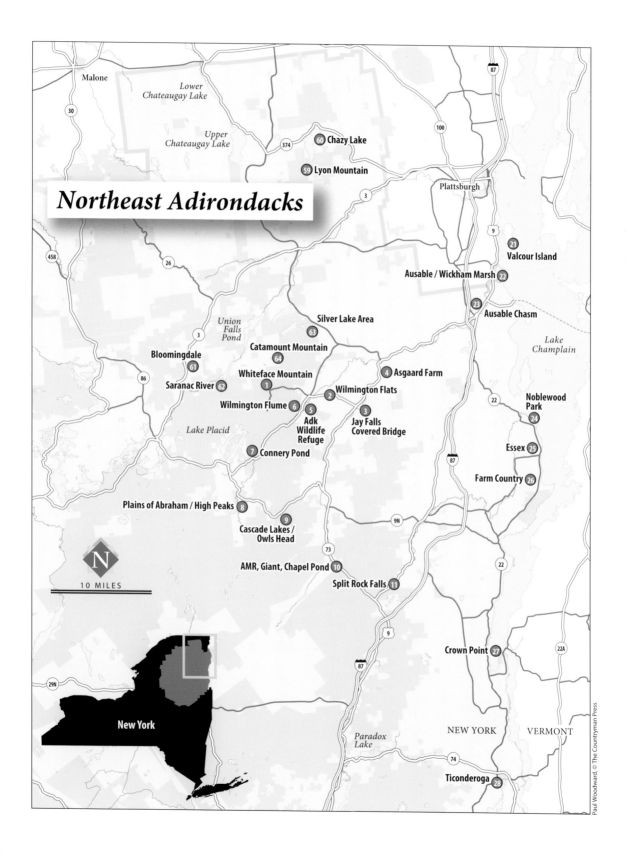

Northeast Adirondacks

Malone

Lower Chateaugay Lake

Upper Chateaugay Lake

60 Chazy Lake

59 Lyon Mountain

Plattsburgh

21 Valcour Island

Ausable / Wickham Marsh 22

23

Ausable Chasm

Lake Champlain

Union Falls Pond

Silver Lake Area

63

Bloomingdale 61

Catamount Mountain 64

4 Asgaard Farm

Whiteface Mountain 1

Saranac River 62

Wilmington Flats 2

Noblewood Park 24

Wilmington Flume 6 5

3 Jay Falls Covered Bridge

Essex 25

Lake Placid

Adk Wildlife Refuge

7 Connery Pond

Farm Country 26

Plains of Abraham / High Peaks 8

9 Cascade Lakes / Owls Head

AMR, Giant, Chapel Pond 10

Split Rock Falls 11

Crown Point 27

New York

Paradox Lake

NEW YORK   VERMONT

Ticonderoga 28

N

10 MILES

New York

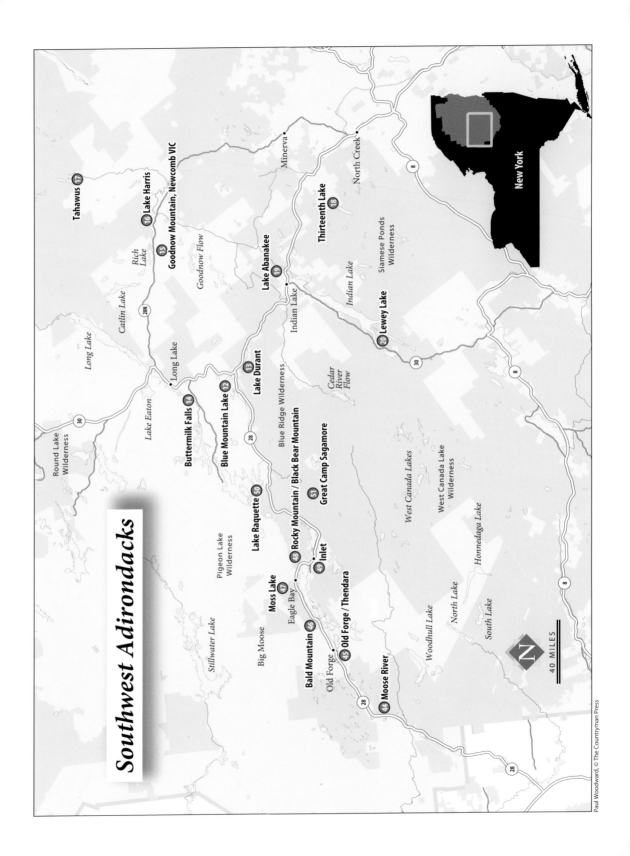

Southwest Adirondacks

New York

N
40 MILES

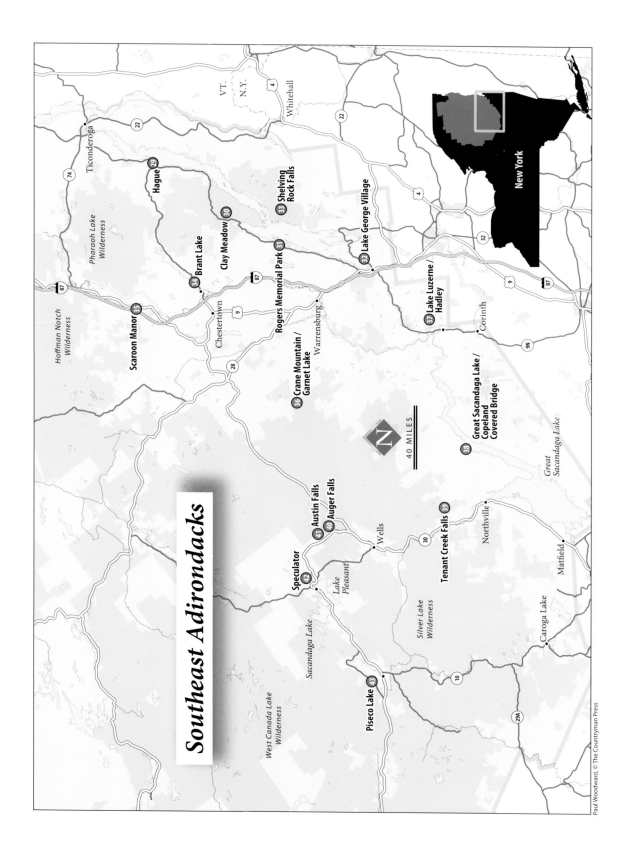

Southeast Adirondacks

40 MILES

New York

VT.
N.Y.

Whitehall

Ticonderoga

Pharaoh Lake Wilderness

Hoffman Notch Wilderness

29 Hague

30 Clay Meadow

33 Shelving Rock Falls

Brant Lake

34

31 Rogers Memorial Park

32 Lake George Village

35 Scaroon Manor

Chestertown

Warrensburg

Corinth

37 Lake Luzerne / Hadley

36 Crane Mountain / Garnet Lake

38 Great Sacandaga Lake / Copeland Covered Bridge

Great Sacandaga Lake

Austin Falls

41

40 Auger Falls

Wells

Speculator

42

Lake Pleasant

Sacandaga Lake

39 Tenant Creek Falls

Northville

Matfield

West Canada Lake Wilderness

Silver Lake Wilderness

Caroga Lake

Piseco Lake

43

Paul Woodward, © The Countryman Press

Morning mist by South Inlet on Raquette Lake

Contents

The Ausable River in the Wilmington Flume

IV. Lake George and the
Southeastern Lakes and Mountains

Color can be found everywhere, as in these reflections in the ripples on the Schroon River.

The Lake George region from Cat Mountain

Introduction

For those who think New York State is just one big city, you only need to cross the "Blue Line" to realize how wrong that is. (The Blue Line is the term used in New York State for the boundaries of the Adirondack and Catskill Parks because blue ink was used on state maps when the parks were first drawn.) The Adirondack Park is the largest park in the lower 48 states. There are more than 6 million acres of land within the park boundary—an area that could contain Yellowstone, Yosemite, Everglades, Grand Canyon, and Great Smoky Mountains National Parks combined and still have room left over. This park, which is approximately equivalent to the size of the state of Vermont or Massachusetts, contains the largest area of wilderness east of the Mississippi River.

This region has been in my blood for as long as I can remember. After my grandfather bought property here in the early 1950s, I traveled here with my parents from southern Pennsylvania, and they eventually bought property here as well. After moving here full-time in the early 1970s, I began hiking and exploring the mountains. It was during my first winter hike in the High Peaks, while snowshoeing up and over Algonquin Peak, the second-highest mountain in the state, that I was inspired to pick up a Minolta SRT 101 and some Kodachrome 64 to try to capture on film the sense of wonder I was feeling about the mountains I was exploring. I had a wonderful time experimenting with the photographic process, but it was many rolls of film later before I began to understand the dynamics of composition and light, as well as the principles of the aperture and shutter, and was able to capture images that evoked a sense of place.

Although I've photographed the region for decades, I'm still seeing new angles and places, and I continue to marvel at the diversity of light, moods, textures, and drama found in the Adirondack landscape. I've been back to some locations many times, and almost every trip brings a new dimension to the landscape. With a park so vast, it's really impossible to photograph it all in a lifetime, much less a vacation, so I often try to work in different spots that offer a sense of the whole region.

I've often been asked during my photography workshops and presentations on the Adirondacks about my favorite places here. My answer is generally "Wherever I happen to be at that moment." While some locations are physically more dramatic than others, they all have a wild, rugged Adirondack beauty, and I enjoy every place I've been to equally. The same goes for the seasonal changes here. While fall colors are visually the most spectacular, the subtle colors and moods of spring, the stark contrasts and drama of winter, and summer's blue waters and deep green forested mountains are all special.

My goal in this book is not to create a road map to every good location to photograph in the park; that would take an encyclopedia. My intent is to offer a diverse selection that will help unlock the possibilities, so that each photographer can explore further on his or her own. It generally doesn't take much to find additional photo situations. Just walking a little farther down the trail, going to the next bend in the road, or waiting for the light to change will open up many new possibilities.

The rugged mountain contours we see are what remain after the glaciers from the last ice age carved and scoured the mountains. While the rounded summits in the park aren't as high in elevation as the jagged peaks in the western United States, a number of the highest mountains rise up to several hundred feet above timberline. Mount Marcy, not far from Lake Placid, is the highest mountain in New York at 5,344 feet above sea level. Just 24 miles east of the summit is 125-mile-long Lake Champlain, with a surface elevation of only 95 feet above sea level.

The charm of the Adirondacks comes from the spectacular combination of lakes, mountains, and waterways. The drama comes from the interplay of the four seasons, mixed with weather conditions affecting the region that arrive from places as diverse as the Arctic, the Great Lakes, the continental United States, and the Gulf Stream in the Atlantic Ocean. This mix of weather conditions throughout the year offers unique photographic opportunities.

To really absorb the Adirondack mystique, paddle a wild lake on a moonlit night with loons calling to one another under the amazing canopy of stars. Or view the spectacle of an Adirondack fall—hillsides glowing in "magic hour" light with red, crimson, and gold. Experience the solitude of winter on a remote snowcapped peak, or relax in the spray of a backcountry waterfall, rainbows dancing in the mist. It won't be long before you succumb to the magic elixir known as the Adirondacks.

Using This Book

Catamount Mountain from Taylor Pond

The Adirondack Park contains about a 50-50 mix of both private land and state-owned land. The state-owned land has been afforded "forever wild" protection by a clause in the New York State Constitution and is open to the public. A majority of the private land is owned by timber companies that maintain the land for timber production rather than development, helping to preserve the wild character of the park. Some of these large landholdings also have recreation easements, allowing hiking, canoeing, and possibly some camping options. It's important to check for specific land use regulations before entering any land open to the public. There are also state campground facilities within the park, in addition to many private campgrounds in villages and hamlets throughout the park.

I have organized the book by starting with the centrally located High Peaks region and then working clockwise around the park. The book includes all the maps and information needed to access each listed location. There are also five topographical National Geographic "Trails Illustrated" maps (www.natgeo maps.com/ti_newyork) that cover the entire park. They show all the public trails, state land, and boat launches, and they also have pertinent reference information. Note that most of the state campgrounds remove their signs along the road once they are closed for the season.

The photo possibilities in the park are endless—from the mountainous High Peaks in the central Adirondacks to the foothills and lakes regions surrounding them. Routes from one photo location to the next often lead past many additional photo ops. You can use this book as a "hit list," but be sure to take advantage of any opportunity you come across—especially if the light is just right. Information on additional events and activities in the region can be found at http://visitadirondacks.com/.

The old saying "A bird in the hand is worth two in the bush" is especially relevant to the Adirondack Park. If the light is great where you are, take advantage of it. This is the East, not the West; photographers don't have perfect photo conditions most times they go out. Take advantage of every great lighting opportunity that comes along. There are always plenty of softer lighting conditions for photographing details. Don't put the camera away just because the light isn't doing what you want. Wander through the big landscapes, pay attention to the details, and tune in to the unique character of the Adirondacks.

Lines and tonal contrasts lead the eye from one subject to another in an image.

Tips for Photographing the Adirondack Park

I generally work with only four basic features on my digital camera—aperture priority mode, shutter priority mode, ISO setting, and exposure compensation. The two shooting modes are used for specific creative options, and the ISO and exposure compensation settings help adjust the exposure. I work in manual mode when I need to use the bulb setting for exposures longer than 30 seconds.

I use aperture priority to set a specific aperture size when depth of field (the amount of the image that will be in sharp focus from near to far) is most important to the image. I use shutter priority when a specific shutter speed is needed to control motion.

Making use of the camera's automatic metering settings allow for greater personal creativity. It helps free the mind so that more thought can go into the composition rather than the settings and camera mechanics. Exposure compensation is a quick way to lighten or darken an exposure. The ISO setting adjusts the sensitivity of the sensor to different intensities of light, but it also affects image quality. The lowest ISO settings create the sharpest, most noise-free images.

Summer sun is great for photographing wide-open landscapes from the mountaintops.

Photographic Principles

The greatest depth of field is achieved with the smallest aperture diameter combined with a short focal length lens. Larger aperture diameters and longer focal lengths offer considerably less depth of field. Adjusting the aperture to maximize or limit the depth of field is the best

The tonal values in a snow scene are much lighter than 18 percent gray, so add about a stop of overexposure compensation to brighten it up if it looks too dark and gray.

way either to draw the eye from a main subject to other details in an image or to emphasize specific details while placing others out of focus.

The faster the shutter speed and the shorter the focal length, the easier it is to stop the action. An easy ratio to remember is to shoot with a shutter speed of at least 1/focal length to keep motion blur to a minimum. For example, if you're working with a 50 mm focal length, the minimum shutter speed needed to stop subtle motion is 1/50 second. When you're working to capture motion blur, use a shutter speed of about 10/focal length—which with a 50 mm lens is 1/5 second. These are simply guidelines; adjust them as necessary to completely stop the action or to show more (or less) motion blur.

Exposure

A camera's light meter averages all of the tonal values in a scene to a neutral 18 percent gray tone. This works well on a typical summer day when the deep blue sky, sunlit green leaves, and lush green grass make for about an 18 percent gray average. But the camera's metering system also tries to average the tones of a snowy field, sandy beach, or foggy morning to an 18 percent gray tone as well. The result is darker than expected tones in the photo.

Exposure compensation is a quick way to correct images that are too dark or too light. Simply dial in some overexposure compensation for any image that appears too dark, or use underexposure compensation for an image that is too light. This is a quick and easy way to brighten up underexposed snow or fog scenes, or to add some zip to the washed-out colors in an overexposed sunset or sunrise. The bottom line is, if the image is too bright, dial in some underexposure and shoot it again.

The camera's histogram shows the various tonal details of each image as a graph. The left side is black; the right is white. If any part of

If colors are too light in an image, try a stop of underexposure compensation to bring out the richness.

the graphed line touches either the black or the white end, parts of the image are pure black or pure white. There is no perfect curve for the graphed line itself. The line simply reflects the abundance of similar tonal values throughout the image. Checking the histogram on each image helps you know if the exposure is close to what you want (whether the main volume of tonal information is either too dark or light), as well as whether the camera was able to capture the full dynamic range of light. The "highlights" feature on the playback menu is a quick and easy way to see which areas are overexposed and clipped to pure white. During image playback, any section of the image with clipped highlights will flash from black to white.

Composition

This is an art, not a science, and every person sees each scene in his or her own way. However, while each composition is personal, it helps if there is an effective tonal balance to the details that help draw the eye throughout the photograph. I work with what I call the contrast evaluation method to create a dynamic balance of energy among all the subjects in a photograph.

Light areas, dark areas, vibrant colors, and lines all tend to attract the eye in a photo. Creating a balance among them helps the eye travel from one subject to another, then another, throughout the image. The "rule of thirds" suggests that the image is divided into thirds vertically and horizontally and that main subjects should be placed near the intersections of the "thirds" lines. This rule is helpful, but the composition still won't work unless there is a dynamic balance of contrasts and colors within the image. Creating an effective tonal balance and working with lines to help guide the eye can also help create a three-dimensional feel within a two-dimensional photograph.

Gear

It's important to put the camera on a tripod anytime depth of field is critical or when you are bracketing (over- and underexposures of the same image) for potential HDR (high-dynamic range) compositing. The main considerations for a good tripod are security and sturdiness, as well as flexibility. It should have independent leg angle locks, and it's best if the

center column can be easily adjusted from vertical to horizontal so the tripod can be used at ground level. A cable release or wireless remote is essential so the shutter can be activated without touching the camera.

I typically carry a full range of focal lengths, from ultrawide to telephoto, a fish-eye lens, and macro equipment. I use fewer filters when shooting digitally, relying on postprocessing and compositing techniques to best re-create what I saw. There are still times when it can be nice to have a split neutral density filter to balance the light in a landscape in high-contrast situations, or to work with a polarizer to cut glare on water or plants. A polarizer can also enhance colors, especially when shooting wet leaves. A solid neutral density filter, either fixed or variable, cuts down the light coming through

Composition is not as much about "thirds" and other "rules" as it is about creating an effective balance of colors, lines, and tonal contrasts.

Left: This wide-angle-lens shot was set up for maximum depth of field. Right: A telephoto lens has less potential depth of field and works well for isolating a subject against a soft background.

the lens, allowing for longer exposures in brightly lit conditions.

When you're working close to the car, most any camera pack will be fine. If you're hiking into the backcountry with a camera, it's important to have a pack that holds the camera equipment you need in addition to hiking gear, food, and water. My latest pack, a Lowepro DryZone Rover, incorporates dry bag technology with enough space to hold a couple of camera bodies, several lenses, hiking gear, and a tripod. It's the best pack I've come across for the backcountry photography I do.

When you're photographing in colder temperatures, taking a warm camera into the cold isn't a problem. However, exposing a cold camera to warm air will cause it to fog up with condensation. If condensation builds up on the inside of the camera, it could kill the electronics. Prevent this by placing the camera in a sealed plastic bag or zipped camera bag before bringing it into a warm space, and keep it enclosed until it warms up to room temperature. If you do find condensation inside a camera, immediately remove the battery. Allow the camera to dry out thoroughly before putting the battery back in, and keep your fingers crossed.

Dress to Stay Dry

For your own personal safety in all kinds of weather, carry along enough layers to stay warm, using synthetic materials for insulation, since they retain a degree of warmth when wet. A synthetic such as PrimaLoft will keep you warm when it gets damp or wet, compared to down, which will compact and lose all insulation value. Do not wear cotton, which is almost impossible to get dry in the field after it's wet and can lead to hypothermia-related issues. Wearing a windproof and waterproof parka and pants over all the layers will block both wind and rain and keep you warm and dry.

A wide-brim waterproof hat or a windproof umbrella (or both) will help you work more comfortably in wet weather conditions. The hat can be used on your head or as a camera cover while you work under the umbrella. Although wet weather photography is not at the top of my favorite things to do list, it does offer some unique photographic opportunities without having to bump elbows with a lot of other people.

Adirondack Light

Weather conditions in the Adirondacks range from as clear and vibrant as you'll ever see to thick pea soup fog in which it's tough to see anything at all. All light is good light; it's just a matter of deciding which subjects and type of imagery work best in the light at hand. Every type of light enhances a subject differently. A general rule of thumb is to photograph the details in the woods and along the streams in soft, overcast conditions and to work the wide-open spaces in brighter, more contrasty light.

"Magic hour" light, when the sun is low in the sky and close to the horizon, is some of the best light for landscapes. Shadows cross the landscape, adding depth and enhancing details, and the light itself takes on a golden glow. Colors become more vibrant, while shadows fill in with the soft light from overhead. These are optimal conditions for shooting and a good time to set up on a ledge or mountaintop or along the edge of a pond or lake. Even magic hour light has different qualities, though, which change with the amount of moisture in the air (the dew point), the number of clouds in the sky, the temperature, and passing warm and cold fronts.

The low angle and warm glow of magic hour light is wonderful for landscape photography.

Fall in the Adirondacks is special, whether you're working the details or the open landscapes.

The Four Seasons

Every season in the Adirondacks has its own charm. Spring is a subtle season, as leaves transition from gentle greens and reds to more vibrant shades of green as they size up on the trees. Trilliums, Dutchman's breeches, spring beauties, and many other early blossoms are scattered through the woods, appearing soon after the snow melts. Pink lady's slippers, plus a couple of other varieties, begin blooming in late May and June. Wild irises decorate wet areas and wild shorelines in mid-June, while various orchids begin to bloom in the bogs scattered throughout the park in mid- to late June.

As the lake waters warm up, fog often builds near dawn, adding mood to the shorelines or becoming a soft undercast carpet of clouds when viewed from a mountain ridge. Fog also appears after summer storms or during a rainy spell, with wisps of clouds and mist floating among the mountains and valleys. Watch for the dramatic light and rainbows that can occur after a storm passes by, especially near sunset.

In late summer the deep green leaves darken before they transition to the vibrant palette of fall colors. Color change is based mostly on elevation differences, with peak color starting in the western Adirondacks and Lake Placid region in late September. The colors gradually spread throughout the rest of the Adirondacks in early to mid-October, with the peak arriving in the Lake Champlain and Lake George basins as late as mid- to late October. Fall brings frosty and sometimes icy mornings, with occasional snowfalls that decorate the fall colors and peaks with a delicate white icing.

Winter comes early and stays late. Snow often covers much of the Adirondacks from Thanksgiving through April, with snowfields on some of the mountain summits lasting into June. Lake Placid has recorded snow on the ground in every month of the year. While the region generally follows a more normal weather pattern, it's good to be prepared for the possibility of some fairly extreme weather changes whenever visiting the Adirondacks.

The Adirondacks are mostly a boreal environment. Fall comes early, winter can be quite harsh with temps well below zero, and spring comes late. Along with spring conditions, which generally arrive in April and May, comes "mud season," as snowmelt and the thawing ground soften dirt roads and trails. This is followed by "bug season," starting with the infamous blackflies, which gradually disappear as the mosquitoes of summer take over. By late July and August, most of the insects have diminished. Conditions just before a rain tend to accentuate insect activity, while clearing and dry air minimize it. Use natural insect repellents, or apply full-strength DEET to a hat or other clothing to help keep annoying insects at bay.

Those few precautions aside, the Adirondacks are one of the most unique landscapes in North America. No matter how long you are here, there is always a new place to explore, and the photo possibilities are endless.

Winter brings a different drama and beauty to the Adirondack Park.

Lake Placid and Whiteface Mountain

I. Lake Placid and the High Peaks Region

Where: Located more or less centrally in the Adirondack Park.
Noted for: Mountain views, lakes, and various sporting events.
Best Time: Fall colors peak around the end of September and early October.
Facilities: None at parking areas or trailheads except at the Adirondak Loj and the castle at the end of the Whiteface Veterans Memorial Highway toll road.
Sleeps and Eats: Lake Placid has many lodging and meal choices. There are additional choices in the towns throughout the region.

General Description: With a mix of beautiful lakes, ponds, and rivers, plus the highest mountains in the state, this region contains some of the most dramatic destinations in the Adirondack Park. The eclectic village of Lake Placid, situated near Whiteface Mountain, hosted the Winter Olympics in 1932 and 1980 and features world-class sports events throughout the year.

Directions: From the Adirondack Northway (I-87), head west on NY 73 from Exit 30 or south on NY 9N from Exit 34. From the west, use NY 30 or 3 to Saranac Lake, then head east on NY 86 to Lake Placid.

Specifically: Ausable Forks, Jay, Keene, Keene Valley, Lake Placid, Wilmington.

1. Whiteface Mountain

Driving up Whiteface Veterans Memorial Highway and taking the elevator to the 4,867-foot-high summit tower on Whiteface Mountain is the easiest way to access the spectacular view from the fifth-highest peak in New York.

Lake Placid from the summit of Whiteface Mountain

There are great views to the High Peaks, Lake Placid, the Saranac Lakes, Lake Champlain, and Vermont from the narrow summit and from the walkway that leads from the summit back down to the magnificent stone castle at the summit parking area. Please walk on bare rock whenever you're wandering around to help protect the alpine vegetation. The growing season is quite short at this altitude, and it can take years for these fragile plants to recover from carelessly placed steps.

Since Whiteface stands alone and is 3,300 feet higher than much of the surrounding land, it is often shrouded in clouds or mist. I've been on Whiteface three times when the conditions were right for the Brocken specter and the surrounding glory. This requires clear, bright sunlight at a fairly low angle and summit mist or clouds opposite the sun. Stand on a rocky point with the sun at your back, and it may be possible to see your ghostly shadow on the clouds, surrounded by a circular rainbow.

Driving the toll road doesn't allow for sunrise or sunset opportunities, since the gates are open only 9–5:30 during the summer and 9–4 in the spring and fall. Hiking and bicycling in these seasons, or cross-country skiing in the winter, allows access when the toll road is closed. There are three hiking trails to the summit. Two of the trailheads are along the south side of the toll road before reaching the tollhouse, and another trail heads up from Whiteface Landing at the north end of Lake Placid (see Connery Pond and Little Cherry Patch Pond [7]). Current tolls are $10 per car and driver plus $6 for each passenger; bicycles are $6. For more information, go to www.whiteface.com.

Directions: From the right-angle turn on NY 86 at the intersection in Wilmington, follow the signs for Whiteface Veterans Memorial Highway. It's about 3 miles to the alpine-style tollhouse by Lake Stevens (with a short nature trail) and another 5 miles to the parking lot, castle, elevator, and walkway. There are a number of pullouts with views along the toll road to the elevator and stone castle at the summit parking area.

2. Wilmington Plains

Along NY 86, about halfway between the towns of Wilmington and Jay, is a half-mile stretch of highway with a wonderful panoramic view of the Sentinel Range and Whiteface

Mountain. There are great views along the length of the open section, plus there is a nicely weathered barn at the far east end to enhance the foreground. Since this view faces south, morning light falls on Whiteface, shadowing the Sentinels, while late afternoon and evening light shadows Whiteface. Please remember to respect private property and stay near the shoulder of the road.

Directions: This view is along NY 86, 3 miles east of the intersection with Whiteface Veterans Memorial Highway in Wilmington, and about 2.25 miles west of the intersection of NY 86 and 9N in Jay. The safest parking is on the north side of 86, opposite the view, in a couple of small pullouts.

3. Jay Falls and Covered Bridge

The restored covered bridge in Jay sits high above the East Branch of the Ausable River, just below Jay Falls, where the river cascades for about 300 feet over a number of ledges into many pools before flowing gently under the bridge. This location has both classic views and unique photo options.

The covered bridge can be photographed from the new bridge a short distance downriver or from the ledges above it. There are wires across the river just upstream of the bridge, so the cleanest view is from downstream. The bridge is lit along the outside at night, making this a great location for twilight shooting, with the bridge softly illuminated in

Whiteface Mountain and other peaks shrouded in clouds in a view from the Wilmington Plains

The restored Jay Bridge over the Ausable River with early fall colors

the first or last light of the day. If it's a hot summer day, be sure to bring along a swimsuit—this is a favorite swimming hole.

Directions: There is parking at both ends of the covered bridge. From the intersection of NY 86 and 9N in Jay, head downhill on Mill Hill Road to the small parking area at the west end of the bridge. If this lot is full, head north on John Fountain Road and turn right on Glen Road. Cross the river on the new bridge, take the first right, and drive to the parking area near the other end of the covered bridge.

4. Asgaard Farm

The views to the mountains from Asgaard Farm have been made famous by the well-known painter and writer Rockwell Kent, who lived at the farm from the 1920s until he died in 1971. This is still a working dairy farm, with open fields and wonderful views to Whiteface, the Sentinels, and a few of the High Peaks farther south. Please note the Private Property signs and stay along the shoulder of the road to photograph.

There are panoramic photo opportunities here, plus there may be wildflowers at the edge of the fields in mid- to late summer. A telephoto lens is best for photographing the distant mountains and farm, while a wide-angle lens works nicely for photographing nearby flowers with the farm and mountains as a backdrop. The views are best when there is good clarity to the air so the most distant mountains are visible, though a very slight haze can add a bluish touch to them. This is a south-facing view, so both morning and evening are nice. Bright sunny conditions can be good as well—with or without clouds over the mountains.

View over Asgaard Farm with a backdrop of mountain peaks and clouds

Ausable River

Directions: Heading north on NY 9N into Ausable Forks, turn right on the Broad Street bridge where 9N makes a left on Main Street. Turn right on Sheldrake Road immediately after crossing the bridge. It's about 1.2 miles to Asgaard Farm; go past the farm entrance to the first views over the fields, just past the pines. Note that it's easy to be sidetracked by the view and not notice the poison ivy growing along the road. The farm's store hours are posted at the farm and online (www.asgaardfarm.com) if you'd like to sample some of its award-winning cheeses or other organic products.

5. Adirondack Wildlife Refuge

This wildlife refuge and rehabilitation center just south of Wilmington features various raptors and mammals, including wolves, owls, hawks, a bald eagle, and many other birds and animals. It is open to the public 10–4 daily and has raptor presentations at 11 AM, 1 PM, and 3 PM. This is a great way to get close-up views of the birds and to learn about them as well. There is no entrance fee, but this a not-for-profit group that survives on donations.

I've used my 70–200 mm zoom for most of the photos I've taken here. Work with an aperture large enough to blur the background, but small enough to keep details in the critter. During a presentation, most of the birds are held outside their cages, which affords good opportunities for photos with a backdrop of trees and leaves.

Directions: From the intersection of NY 86 and Whiteface Veterans Memorial Highway in Wilmington, head east about 0.5 mile on 86. Turn right (south) on Springfield Road (County Route 12). The Adirondack Wildlife Refuge sign and driveway are 1 mile on the right. Drive to the large parking lot on the right. It's a short walk down the driveway to the refuge. For more information, go to www .adirondackwildlife.org.

6. Wilmington Flume and Ausable River

Here the wild Ausable River is channeled into a steep-sided gorge, where it plunges over a couple of sets of waterfalls. The water begins to narrow and drop over ledges on the west wide of NY 86 and exits the flume some 1,200 feet later on the east side of the highway. There are trails on both sides of the river along the gorge, as well as on the north and west sides by the parking area right by the bridge.

This is a local swimming hole that's great for photography on cloudy, misty days, when it's less likely there will be swimmers. On sunny days it can also be fun to photograph the swimmers jumping off the ledges into the frothy water below the waterfalls. Use a fast shutter speed of 1/500 or more to stop their action.

There are many other scenic places to photograph the river for the next several miles south of here, as it winds its way through Wilmington Notch and along NY 86. High Falls Gorge has maintained trails, bridges, and walkways to provide access to another gorge and beautiful waterfalls. This section of the Ausable River, renowned for its "trophy trout," is subject to special fishing regulations and has the potential for some great fishing photos.

Directions: The flume is along NY 86, 2 miles south of the intersection of 86 and Whiteface Veterans Memorial Highway in Wilmington— just before the Hungry Trout. There are two parking areas for the flume. One is on the west side by the bridge over the river, and the other is a paved pullout on the east side, a short distance north of the bridge. Follow the trails on the northeast, southeast, and northwest sides to various vantage points.

7. Connery Pond and Little Cherry Patch Pond

The view to Whiteface Mountain is an Adirondack classic. While morning light is best, you can find great photos all day. The short trail from the parking area leads to a reed-filled sandy shore by the small outlet stream. The right conditions bring rose-colored mist rising from the water, with Whiteface standing majestically above the distant shore. Please use care when walking so as not to trample vegetation more than is necessary. It can be rather muddy as you get closer to the lake.

Directions: From the intersection of NY 73 and 86 in Lake Placid, head east on 86. In about 0.5 mile there is a great view to the ski jumps and High Peaks from the edge of the golf course. At 2.6 miles there is a wonderful view on the left over Little Cherry Patch Pond to Whiteface. At 2.9 miles there is a dirt road on the left with a small trail sign for Whiteface Landing. Park here or drive in 0.7 mile to the small parking area on the right. The trail is just to the left of the parking area.

8. Plains of Abraham and the High Peaks

Just east of the ski jumps near Lake Placid are the Plains of Abraham along NY 73 and Adirondak Loj Road. There are great views all along the first mile of the latter. If you can manage to put the camera away and make it past this section, drive into the parking area at the Adirondak Loj ($10 per car, $5 for Adirondack Mountain Club members) to the most popular access point for the High Peaks.

A short walk to the eastern and northern shores of Heart Lake offers some stunning views south to Algonquin and other peaks.

Morning mist and colors at Connery Pond

The steep half-mile climb (Short Trail) up Mount Jo offers some of the finest views in the Adirondacks for the least climbing effort. Longer hikes lead past Marcy Dam (2.1 miles) to the wild, rugged U-shaped valley of Avalanche Pass (3.5 miles) and Lake Colden Dam (5 miles). A strenuous mountain hike goes past a waterfall to the dramatic views above timberline from the summit of Algonquin Peak (4 miles). Longer still is the hike to the rocky summit of Mount Marcy (7.5 miles), the highest peak in New York. You'll pass the trailhead for Mount Van Hoevenberg on the way in to the Loj. This mountain (2.2 miles) has wonderful views over South Meadow to the panorama of the High Peaks on the horizon. These are all highly recommended destinations if you enjoy photographing in the backcountry.

Directions: Adirondak Loj Road is on the south side of NY 73, 3.3 miles southeast of the intersection of NY 73 and 86 in Lake Placid. Follow Adirondak Loj Road 3.7 miles to a dirt road on the left. The Van Hoevenberg trailhead is a short distance up the dirt road. Past the dirt road, at 4.7 miles, is the parking area for the High Peaks Information Center. There are numerous No Parking signs along Adirondak Loj Road near the information center. Cars parked here are regularly ticketed.

9. Cascade Lakes, Cascade Mountain, Pitchoff Mountain, and Owls Head

Here are a waterfall, Upper and Lower Cascade Lakes, and three great climbs that have nearby trailheads. Cascade Mountain, at 4,098 feet, has one of the finest views from the top of any of the 4,000-plus-foot High Peaks and is also one of the shortest to climb (2.5 miles). It's a good place to be any time of the day when there is a view and is especially impressive in magic hour light. On Pitchoff Mountain, the "balanced rock" ledges have a fine westerly view (1.5 miles), plus there are good views

View from along Adirondak Loj Road over the Plains of Abraham

from several points along the rugged ridge to the fifth summit (3.6 miles).

Afternoon light or soft, cloudy-day light can be best for the Cascade Lakes views, since the lakes are shadowed in the morning. There's a great view down the lakes to Algonquin Peak from the far east end of the lakes, plus other views from pullouts along NY 73. The picnic area between the lakes has views of the waterfall from above the parking area; there is a short trail to the base of the falls.

Rare calm morning light on Lower Cascade Lake

About a mile east of the lakes is Owls Head Mountain. It's only a half mile to the rocky summit, with views from open ledges starting about halfway up.

Directions: Trailhead parking for Cascade and Pitchoff Mountains is along NY 73, 6.6 miles west of the Y intersection of 73 and NY 9N in Keene. At 0.75 mile east of this trailhead, a small road on the right drops steeply downhill to the picnic area between the lakes. There are additional pullouts along the lake (for rock climbers on the cliffs) when heading east of this road. At 3.5 miles east of the trailhead is Owls Head Road. The Owls Head Mountain trailhead is about a 0.25-mile drive on the dirt road.

10. Chapel Pond, Giant Mountain, and Adirondack Mountain Reserve

Just several miles from the Adirondack Northway (I-87) is another wonderful collection of locations to shoot. The beautiful clear waters of Chapel Pond are right along the road, at times perfectly reflecting the cliffs at the base of Round Mountain across the pond. There is parking by the central area of the pond, as well as at the east end. At the far east end of the Giant Mountain trailhead parking, a pretty stream bubbles over cobblestones and past steep ledges before flowing into Chapel Pond.

There are special views of the mountains along the Giant Ridge Trail from ledges just a half mile from NY 73, as well as from many other spots along the open-ridge sections of this strenuous, rugged trail to the summit of Giant Mountain (3.5 miles). I often scout out the views on the way up and plan to be at different locations for evening magic hour light on the way back down, but take advantage of any good light you find.

Just down the hill from Chapel Pond is a pullout with a view of three-tier, 100-foot-high Roaring Brook Falls to the right (north). At the bottom of the hill is the trailhead for both the top and bottom of the falls. There are various photo possibilities at the bottom, as well as nice views from the top.

Across NY 73 from the falls trailhead is parking for Adirondack Mountain Reserve (AMR) land. Noonmark Mountain is a favorite hike of mine, and Round Mountain is a close second. Both have great but different views of the surrounding peaks. Each is a strenuous 2.5-mile climb from the parking area. Just uphill on the dirt road from the two trailheads is a view to Giant Mountain over the Ausable Club golf course, which doesn't require any climbing! From the main AMR trailhead, accessible by the private road to Lower Ausable Lake, the West River Trail offers many photo options as it meanders along the East Branch Ausable River on its way to 60-foot-high Beaver Meadow Falls (3.5 miles). Another great climb is the photogenic Gill Brook Trail to Indian Head, where there are spectacular views over the Ausable Lakes and surrounding mountains (4 miles). Rainbow Falls, near the outlet of Lower Ausable Lake, drops about 150 feet almost straight down into a narrow gorge. This is really special to see. Lighting contrasts can

A long exposure of evening twilight from the summit of Giant Mountain

be a bit tough here, so it can be a good place to play with bracketing and HDR techniques.

Directions: From Exit 30 on the Northway (I-87) head west on NY 73 about 6 miles to the paved Giant Ridge Trail parking area along both sides of the road. Parking for Chapel Pond is on the left at 6.2 miles, at the central part of the pond. The paved overlook for the falls is on the right at 6.3 miles, and the parking lots for the Roaring Brook Falls Trail (right) and AMR (left) are at 6.5 miles, at the base of a steep hill.

11. Split Rock Falls

There are some great angles looking toward the falls, as well as views from the top of them, both of which are easily accessible from the roadside parking area. Cloudy or misty soft light helps bring out all the details and textures in the weathered rock walls around the base of the falls, while warm summer days bring out the swimmers who love to jump into the pool there.

Directions: From the crazy intersection of US 9 and NY 73, 2.2 miles west of Exit 30 on the Northway (I-87), head 2.3 miles north on US 9 to the paved parking area on the right. Short footpaths lead downhill to the bottom of the falls, and the top of the falls is just uphill from the lot.

Pro Tips: Most people want to get to the top of the highest mountain, but the best views are often from the smaller mountains or ledges looking toward the higher mountains. Lots of light and cloud conditions can work for mountain photography, but the best light is still the magic hour light. About the only way to take advantage of that is to hike in—or out—with a headlamp so you can be on location at the magic hour.

Changing weather, especially clearing after a rain, can create all kinds of moods and lighting. It's really tough to predict what will happen in changing weather; you simply have to be there to be able to see it and photograph it. Mountaintops are a great place to shoot panoramas. It's best to shoot a series of images for panoramic stitching with the camera perpendicular to the orientation of the view; overlap the images by at least 30 percent.

Cautions: Backcountry trails here can be rugged and steep. Be fully prepared for whatever weather the mountains might offer. It's suggested that you hike in a group of at least four people and stay within your comfort zone. Know the symptoms of hypothermia. Carry plenty of water and extra food, and wear synthetics for all layers. Don't wear cotton, which gets wet easily, stays damp a long time, and is the leading cause of hypothermia-related problems. Always carry a windproof and waterproof parka and pants for full protection. Many locations in the mountains are out of cell phone range, and a GPS unit might not work in mountain valleys. Be sure to have a map and compass as a backup, and know how to navigate with them.

Diversions: While in the area, you might want to visit Lake Placid's Olympic venues. At the Olympic Center, the underdog U.S. men's hockey team beat the Russians to win the gold medal at the 1980 Olympics, and Eric Heiden won an unprecedented five gold medals on the adjacent skating oval that's in front of the school. There are also the ski jumps, the Mount Van Hoevenberg bobsled run, and the lift ride up Whiteface. Located just outside town near the ski jumps are abolitionist John Brown's photogenic historic home and barns. If you need any backcountry gear, check out the Mountaineer in Keene Valley or High Peaks Cyclery, Jones Outfitters, or Eastern Mountain Sports in Lake Placid. An easy way to stay up-to-date on area sporting events is to visit www.lakeplacid.com.

Split Rock Falls

Crescent moon and Venus from the Lake Durant campground beach

II. Central Lakes and Mountains

General Description: Here you'll find beautiful lakes, waterways, waterfalls, and smaller mountains, plus access to the southern High Peaks. There are a number of roadside destinations, a few climbs, and plenty of places to access with a canoe. This section includes the wild Hudson River Gorge, a premier destination for white-water rafting and paddling.

Directions: This area is reached from Exits 25 through 29 on the Adirondack Northway (I-87). Or head south on NY 30 from Tupper Lake, east on NY 28 from Old Forge, or north on NY 28 from the Warrensburg area.

Specifically: Blue Mountain Lake, Indian Lake, Long Lake, Newcomb, North Creek, North River.

12. Blue Mountain Lake

A favorite photo location in town is at Curry's Cottages, where through the summer and fall a number of white Adirondack chairs are lined up along the shore—against a backdrop of the lake and mountains. This spot is just to the right of the public beach and canoe launch area, which also has some views overlooking Blue Mountain Lake. Please remember that the chairs are on private property. Ask at the office for permission to get closer. (The owners will appreciate receiving photos of what you shoot.) A telephoto lens can capture some nice angles, and the chairs look good in all kinds of light. Sunset is on the opposite side of the lake, so this area can provide some excellent photo ops when the setting sun lights up clouds over the water.

The open ledge at the top of Castle Rock has a beautiful 180-degree south-facing view of Blue Mountain on the left, the lake just left

Where: The central Adirondacks, to the south of the High Peaks.
Noted for: Mountain, lake, and river views.
Best Time: Fall colors peak from late September to early October.
Facilities: In season by the beaches in Blue Mountain Lake, Long Lake, and Newcomb (Lake Harris); at the Adirondack Interpretive Center (Newcomb); and at Lake Harris and Lake Durant state campgrounds.
Sleeps and Eats: North Creek has year-round lodging and meals and a grocery store. Much of the lodging throughout the rest of this area is seasonal.

of center, and the foothill mountains off to the right. Evening light is perhaps best, since Blue Mountain is shadowed in the morning. Misty morning light, with fog rising off the lake in the early sunlight, is quite nice as well. It's a moderately strenuous 1.5-mile hike to the ledge.

Blue Mountain also has some wonderful views from the summit fire tower overlooking Blue Mountain Lake and the lakes region to the west, with the High Peaks on the horizon to the northeast. Magic hour light and fairly clear air help set off this panoramic view. It's a rather strenuous 2-mile hike to the fire tower from the trailhead.

Directions: The town beach and chairs are along NY 28, 0.25 mile west of the T intersection of NY 28 and 28N/30. The Blue Mountain trailhead is 1.4 miles north of the T on 28N/30 at the top of the hill on the right. For Castle Rock, from the T head north on 28N/30 to the Maple Lodge Road/Minnowbrook Conference Center turnoff on the left at 0.6 mile.

Blue Mountain and Blue Mountain Lake from Castle Rock

It's another 1.3 miles to the trailhead at the conference center, at the end of the road.

13. Lake Durant

There are lots of options for shooting around this state-owned Adirondack lake, with the two easiest being right along the main road, across from the parking area, and along the old road that follows the shoreline, also across from the parking area. This old road divides the lake and the marsh. I've seen otters, herons, loons, and beavers, and I'm sure there's lots of other wildlife around the lake as well.

Sunset light and twilight can be quite nice from the beach area of the campground at the east end of the lake. Either walk in from the trail that leads south across the lake's outlet dam, from the Northville Placid Trail parking area along the south side of NY 28/30, or pay the day-use fee at the state campground and drive in. The campground area also has different views across the lake to Blue Mountain. These are especially pleasing a short distance beyond the beach area where a stream enters the lake. Sunrise light can be impressive from the lake access at the end of the dirt road at the west end of the lake. Canoeing on the lake lets you explore the small islands and wild shoreline, as well as adjoining Rock Pond.

Directions: From the T intersection of NY 28 and 28N/30 in Blue Mountain Lake, head east on 28/30 toward Indian Lake for 0.8 mile to the Y intersection. Bear right on Durant Road. In another 0.2 mile turn left on the dirt road and follow this to the circle by the lake. There are two lake access points here.

The parking area and old road around the lakeshore are along NY 28/30, 1.6 miles east of the T in Blue Mountain Lake. The Northville Placid Trail parking area is 2.6 miles east of the T, and the campground entrance is 3 miles from the T.

14. Buttermilk Falls

By the falls, the Raquette River is the drainage for three major lakes plus many smaller ones, so there's always a good water flow coming over the falls. I've been here in all seasons, at different times of day, and in various weather conditions, and I always find something new to photograph.

The long sloping cascade of water ends with about a 20-foot drop. There are many options for shooting across the quiet water at the head of the falls, along the cascade, and beside and below the drop. In early spring there are fiddleheads, followed by flowers and ferns. Intertwined cedar roots stabilize the shore, and there's a rocky shoal and small island at the bottom that offer various perspectives. Look for some great reflections when the sun is shining on the trees on the far shore and the nearby water is in shadow.

Cedars and bluets at the base of Buttermilk Falls

Directions: From the T intersection of NY 28 and 28N/30 in Blue Mountain Lake, head north on 28N/30. At 7.7 miles, immediately after the S-curve, turn left on North Point Road. Travel another 2.1 miles to the parking area on the right at the sign for the falls. It's a very short walk on the trail to the falls.

Valley mist and the High Peaks in morning light from the Goodnow Mountain fire tower

15. Goodnow Mountain and the Adirondack Interpretive Center

The restored fire tower on the top of Goodnow Mountain has great views overlooking the lakes and High Peaks to the north, as well as other surrounding lakes and mountains. Light can be good at both sunset and sunrise, as well as when clouds are stacked up over the mountains or when the valleys are cloaked in fog. Telephoto focal lengths can be helpful to bring out the details in the mountains, but there are some striking panoramas from the tower as well. It's a moderately strenuous 2-mile hike to the summit from the trailhead.

The Adirondack Interpretive Center, with nature trails along Rich Lake, is just east of the Goodnow trailhead. The 3.6 miles of nature trails pass through some old-growth forest, and there are nice views and the potential for seeing wildlife along these easily accessible trails.

Directions: From the T intersection of NY 28N and 30 in Long Lake, drive north and east toward Newcomb on 28N. It is 10.4 miles to the Goodnow Mountain trailhead parking lot on the right (south) side of the road. The Adirondack Interpretive Center is 10.9 miles from the T, on the left (north).

16. Lake Harris

Morning light over the mountains and shore, with a soft mist rising from the water, can make this the perfect Adirondack shot. Lake Harris is roughly centered in the town of Newcomb. There are two access sites, a town beach on the south side and a state campground on the northeast shore. In a canoe it's an easy paddle from the town beach to the state land on the north shore, as well as to the outlet to the Hudson River at the east end of the lake. This is a busy place on a hot summer day, but a great place for colors and reflections on a calm fall day.

Morning light on Lake Harris

Directions: From the T intersection of NY 28N and 30 in Long Lake, it is 14.7 miles on 28N to Beach Road in Newcomb. Turn left on Beach Road and drive the short distance to the parking area to access the town park. NY 28N crosses the Hudson River at 15.6 miles, with views south to Vanderwhacker Mountain. Campsite Road is on the left at about 16 miles. It's just under 2 miles to the state campground area.

17. Tahawus

The Tahawus area was a thriving iron mining community in the early to mid-1800s. The titanium dioxide in the rock made it difficult to extract the iron ore, however, so the mines closed. They reopened in 1940, this time for the titanium, and operated until 1989. It's possible they will begin operation again soon. The blast furnace and some of the early buildings are still standing, including MacNaughton Cottage, where Vice President Theodore Roosevelt was staying in 1901 when he learned that President William McKinley had been shot. Some of these structures are undergoing restoration. There are some interesting photo ops around the "ghost buildings."

The Tahawus area also provides the main access to the southern High Peaks, Henderson Lake, and Mount Adams. Henderson Lake is set among some smaller mountains, with views to the larger mountains from out on the water.

The best views are either from a canoe or from shoreline areas accessed by a canoe. The only trail near the lake leads 0.5 mile from the trailhead to the boat launch. One of the more dramatic views is from the main part of the lake looking north to Algonquin Peak, Mount Marshall, and Wallface Mountain, with its craggy rock face. Wallface has the highest wilderness cliff in the Northeast. A telephoto lens helps accentuate the size of these somewhat distant higher mountains, while keeping the lake in the foreground. Use a small enough aperture to gain the depth of field needed to have both in sharp focus.

The fire tower on top of Mount Adams has one of the finest panoramic views of the High Peaks from the south. It's well worth the rather strenuous 2.4-mile hike from the trailhead to the summit to see this fabulous view. Evening light is perhaps best here when the summer sun casts shadows across the peaks. But any time of the day can be nice with clouds skimming over the summits.

Directions: From NY 28N turn left (north) on Blue Ridge Road about 5 miles east of Newcomb. There is a Department of Environmental Conservation (DEC) High Peaks Wilderness sign at the intersection. Continue straight (north) at the first Y at 0.25 mile. Bear left (north) on Tahawus Road at the second Y at 1.25 miles, where the right fork leads to North Hudson. Bear left again on Upper Works Road at 7.6 miles, by the Hikers sign, just before the bridge over a narrow section of Sanford Lake. The rough, winding road will pass by upper Sanford Lake and then the old stone blast furnace, just before reaching the Mount Adams trailhead. The ghost buildings are near the trailhead at the end of the road. It's 11 miles from 28N to the Hanging Spear Falls/Mount Adams trailhead and 11.5 miles to the Henderson Lake trailhead at the end of the road.

A Hornbeck canoe beached along the shore of Henderson Lake

Peaked Mountain and fall foliage from the edge of a beaver pond along the trail to the summit

18. Thirteenth Lake

This pretty lake located at the northeast corner of the remote Siamese Ponds Wilderness has a couple of access points. The water is only a short distance from the northern trailhead parking and boat launch area. It's about a 1-mile walk from the trailhead on the east side of the lake. The view from the eastern shore looks across the water to the mountains on the other side. Since this is a north-south lake, the mountains are lit up in morning light and shadowed in the afternoon. Canoeing around this beautiful wild lake opens up many photo options. Please respect the private property along the northeast shore of the lake.

The trail to Peaked Mountain follows the northwest shore before heading up along a photogenic stream that flows from Peaked Mountain Pond. There are a couple of small beaver flows that might have some great reflections, especially at the peak of fall foliage in early October. Peaked Mountain Pond, reached at 2.5 miles, mirrors Peaked Mountain on a calm day. The summit ledges, 3 miles from the trailhead, have some great views south and west overlooking the Siamese Ponds Wilderness.

Directions: From NY 28 in North River, travel 3.3 miles west on Thirteenth Lake Road to the Y. Bear right for the boat access trailhead (0.8 mile) and the Peaked Mountain Trail. To access the east side of the lake, bear left at the Y and follow the signs to the Old Farm trailhead at 1.7 miles.

19. Indian River

Just east of the village of Indian Lake, a dam backs up the Indian River, forming Lake Abanakee. On the river below the dam is an access point for rafters and kayakers heading to the Hudson River and the whitewater in the Hudson River Gorge. A dirt road parallels the river below the dam, providing a number of access points for photographers. Misty morning light creates a great mood for the river at the rafting access point. Farther downstream, from midmorning until about noon, there are usually some fun, colorful photo ops of the rafters and kayakers who ride the midmorning water release.

Directions: From the T intersection of NY 28 and 30 in Indian Lake, head east on 28, past Byron Park, for 1.3 miles to Chain Lakes Road, which is just before the bridge over Lake Abanakee. Head north about 1.5 miles to the parking area for rafters. It's a short walk down the hill to the river. The road gets quite close to a section of rapids in another 0.75 mile, offering some white-water photo ops.

20. Lewey Lake Area

In addition to the potential for photos along the road, this area offers direct access to Lewey Lake at the state campground and to Indian Lake at the boat launch on the north side of the road. There are photo possibilities from the shoreline and the campground beach, as well as great views of Lewey Mountain and Snowy Mountain from out on both Lewey Lake and Indian Lake. The Miami River flows into the south end of Lewey Lake. It's a satisfying paddle, with some quick portages over beaver dams, views of the landscape, and the potential to photograph wildlife. I've seen blue herons and mergansers almost every time I've been in this area.

Mason Lake, 4.25 miles south of the campground entrance, is a nice place to catch sunset light. Wander out on the unmarked footpath on the left side of the parking area to some lake-level views only a few hundred feet from your car.

Morning mist over Lake Abanakee

Fall colors along the Miami River at the south end of Lewey Lake

Directions: From the T intersection of NY 28 and 30 in Indian Lake, drive 12 miles south on 30 to the Lewey Lake state campground on the right (south) and the Indian Lake boat launch on the left (north).

Pro Tips: There are a lot of hardwood forests throughout this area, which are great for fall colors around the beginning of October. Trees in the wetlands peak a week or more before those on the hillsides, with vibrant reds, yellows, and oranges.

Cautions: Be aware of changing water levels along the Indian River, as water is released for the rafting companies (daily April through mid-June; Tuesday through Thursday, Saturday, and Sunday mid-June through Labor Day; Saturday and Sunday only after Labor Day). Keep a close eye on the weather when paddling on Indian Lake. A strong north wind blowing down the length of this lake can kick up some big waves.

Diversions: Gore Mountain offers summer and fall gondola rides to the top of 3,200-foot Bear Mountain, with good views of the Gore Mountain summit and surrounding mountains. North Creek is also home to the North Creek Railroad, offering various photo ops from its scenic tours along the wild Hudson River from Saratoga to North Creek (daily in season). To see and photograph the Hudson River Gorge close-up, check out the rafting companies in the North Creek/North River area. Be sure to have a dry bag or waterproof housing for your camera. Snowy Mountain is along NY 30, south of Indian Lake. The strenuous 4-mile hike to the restored fire tower on the summit traverses some open ledges along the way. The panoramic summit view is best to the north and east—good for sunrise light over the lake and mountains and late afternoon light.

The Ausable Marsh Wildlife Management Area along the edge of Lake Champlain, with a Hornbeck canoe beached on the sand

III. The Champlain Valley

General Description: The Champlain Valley is unique in the Adirondacks, with beautiful open fields rolling over the gentle hills along Lake Champlain. There are great views, a couple of wildlife sites, hiking and canoeing destinations, and historical sites that date to before the Revolutionary War.

Directions: The Champlain Valley is east of US 9, with a boundary of NY 74 and Ticonderoga in the south and Peru in the north. It can be accessed from Exits 28 through 35 on the Adirondack Northway (I-87).

Specifically: Crown Point, Essex, Peru, Keeseville, Ticonderoga, Wadhams, Whallonsburg, Willsboro.

Where: The eastern Adirondacks along Lake Champlain.

Noted for: Rolling foothills, open fields, historical sites, waterfalls, and Lake Champlain.

Best Time: Fall colors peak about the second and third weeks of October.

Facilities: At the Crown Point State Historic Site, Noblewood Park (in season), private campgrounds (during operating hours), and the fishermen's access by Whallon Bay.

Sleeps and Eats: Ticonderoga is the largest town in this area; it and the other larger towns offer lodging and meal options. The city of Plattsburgh, just to the north, has many motels and stores, as well as a mall.

21. Valcour Island

Valcour Island is the northeasternmost point in the Adirondack Park. The easiest access is by boat or canoe from the state boat launch in Peru. There are some great views of the island from the shore, which can include the Green Mountains of Vermont behind the lighthouse from some vantage points along the main road near the boat launch. A telephoto lens is best for this shot on a clear afternoon or evening.

The island is typical Adirondack habitat—rocky, craggy, and tree (and poison ivy) covered. There's an open stony beach on the south side of the island, with views west to the Adirondacks, as well as east across Grand Isle to the Green Mountains in Vermont. Sailboats are often seen plying these waters in the widest section of the lake, which is almost 13 miles wide from the New York shoreline to the far reaches of Malletts Bay in Vermont. If it's a calm day, head just south of Valcour to explore and photograph from Garden Island, a beautiful rocky knoll in the middle of a big expanse of water.

Directions: From Exit 35 on the Northway (I-87), head east 2.9 miles on NY 442 to US 9. Drive north on 9 for another 3.2 miles to the Peru state boat launch.

22. Ausable Marsh and Wickham Marsh Wildlife Management Areas

Just south of the Valcour Island access are two state wildlife management areas bordering Lake Champlain that are just a couple of miles apart. While Ausable Marsh is mostly wetlands, Wickham Marsh has a mix of woodlands and wetlands. Both units have trails and an observation deck, canoeing options, and wildlife viewing, which is best during the spring waterfowl migration. These are also good locations to photograph eagles in the winter before this section of Lake Champlain freezes. Maps for each unit are available at www.dec.ny.gov.

Directions: From Exit 35 on the Northway (I-87), head east 2.9 miles on NY 442 to US 9.

For Ausable Marsh, turn left (north) on US 9 and travel 0.4 mile to Ausable Point Campground Road. Parking for the viewing platform is on the right in another 0.5 mile. For a hiking trail across a dike in the marsh, turn right (south) on US 9 and travel 0.1 mile, then turn left on Ausable Marsh Access Road.

For the north and east sides of Wickham Marsh, take US 9 south 2.8 miles to Giddings Road (Back Road). Head east 1 mile to a small parking area and trailhead on the right or continue 0.5 mile farther to a large parking area on the right with a universally accessible trail and viewing platform. At 1.8 miles Giddings Road turns south and runs along the shore of Lake Champlain. There are several pullout parking areas, a small canoe launch, and a larger parking area and trailhead located along this half-mile stretch of road between the marsh and the railroad bed next to Lake Champlain. To access the south side and interior hiking trails, follow US 9 south to NY 373. Turn left (east) on 373 and travel 1.3 miles to the large Department of Environmental Conservation (DEC) parking area.

23. Ausable Chasm

Since most of the sandstone coverings in the Adirondacks have been stripped away by glaciers and weathering, this almost 2-mile-long sandstone gorge is somewhat of an anomaly in the region. The sheer-walled gorge has trails

Ausable River in the Ausable Chasm

Lake Champlain and the outlet of the Boquet River at Noblewood Park

and walkways that line the rim and also access some of the deepest parts of the gorge. Clouds help reduce the lighting contrasts here, diffusing the light to enhance the subtle details of the rock in the depths of the gorge.

Neighboring Keeseville has some historic stone buildings and bridges, plus an old iron pedestrian bridge just above the park and cascades of Keeseville Falls, which flow by an old factory building in town.

Directions: From Exit 34 on the Northway (I-87), head north on NY 9N into Keeseville. Turn left (north) on US 9 and continue for 1.25 miles to the entrance to Ausable Chasm. For current admission information, check www.ausablechasm.com. To access the falls in town, turn right (south) on NY 22 (Main Street). The bridge below the falls is at the bottom of the hill. To access the pedestrian bridge, park, and ledges along the falls, turn right (south) just past the bridge on US 9/NY 22 (Front Street), then right again in 1 block on Clinton Street.

24. Noblewood Park

Noblewood is a town park just southeast of Willsboro, situated along the Boquet River where it empties into Lake Champlain. This primitive park was created through a partnership between the town of Willsboro and the Adirondack branch of the Nature Conservancy to protect the beautiful floodplain forest along the sandy shoreline. There's a small beach, as well as views from the pavilion and parking area on the hill. You can often see waterfowl here, particularly during the migration, as well as other wildlife. The shoreline ends at a sandy

The Essex Inn, a classic building in historic Essex

spit at the outlet of the river, a short distance north of the beach. There are views across Lake Champlain to Vermont, as well as along New York's Adirondack Park shoreline.

Directions: From the north, take Exit 33 on the Northway (I-87) and travel 10.2 miles south on NY 22, going through Willsboro and reaching the sign for Noblewood Park on the left. From the south, follow the directions for Essex (25), then head north for 3 miles on NY 22 (Lakeshore Road) to the park on the right. There is a day-use fee when the park is open. When it's closed, park by the entrance and walk the short distance to the parking area on the bluff and from there to the shoreline.

25. Essex

A short walk around the historic town of Essex opens up many different photo possibilities,

especially for those who enjoy photographing small-town architecture. The whole town is listed on the National Register of Historic Places, with many buildings dating to the 1800s. The nicely kept homes, buildings, and flower beds around them have a classic New England village character. Beggs Point Park offers great views over Lake Champlain and the neighboring marina. The ferry to Vermont, which you can ride as a passenger or with your car, provides views to both sides of the lake on the 20-minute ride to Vermont. With the right timing, you can photograph the sun setting over the Adirondacks from the top deck of the ferry on the return trip. The ferry and other sites are all within about 3 blocks of the parking area.

Directions: From Exit 31 on the Northway (I-87), head east a few hundred feet and turn left on Youngs Road (County Route 59). Bear right at 2.8 miles on Elizabethtown-Wadhams Road and continue to the intersection with NY 22 at 2.9 miles in Wadhams. You might also want to check out the Boquet River falls by the bridge in Wadhams. Continue on NY 22 to Essex, at 12.2 miles. Turn left at the T at the bottom of the hill. The parking lot is on the left across from the ferry landing.

26. Farm Country

The Champlain Valley farmlands are in a unique location, with the Adirondack High Peaks just to the west and Lake Champlain and Vermont's Green Mountains to the east. There are a number of photo options along the quiet rural roads, with the highest points offering the best views over the fields to the mountains and lake. The open fields may be planted with various crops or used for growing hay. During the summer you may find some of the fields full of hay bales. Wildflowers grow along the roads through much of the summer and fall. Wide-angle lenses can be used to photograph flowers and the landscape behind, while telephoto focal lengths help make the mountains look larger in relation to the foreground. There is nearby access to the Lake Champlain shoreline at Whallon Bay, with a broad view of the lake and Vermont mountains—a great spot for a beautiful sunrise over the lake.

Directions: Follow the directions in the previous entry to NY 22 in Wadhams. Continue on NY 22 to Whallonsburg, then turn right on Whallons Bay Road (County Route 22K) at 6.7 miles. This road heads uphill along the fields to an intersection with Clark and Cross Roads at 7.6 miles. There's a great view west to the High Peaks from the height of land along Clark Road. Continue on Whallons Bay Road to 8.3 miles, where Middle Road (County Route 22M) intersects from the left. Turn left on Middle Road for additional views from different vantage points for the next several miles.

From the intersection with Middle Road continue on Whallons Bay Road to the intersection with Lakeshore Road at 1.3 miles. Turn right (south) for the fishermen's parking area on the right at 1.4 miles. A tunnel under the road a short distance north of the parking area leads down to the shoreline level. Or you can walk down to the shore along the closest section of Albee Road.

Sunrise over Whallon Bay, Lake Champlain

Fields and the High Peaks from Champlain Valley farmland

The new bridge across Lake Champlain at Crown Point

27. Crown Point State Historic Site

The Crown Point State Historic Site contains the stone ruins of Fort Crown Point and Fort St. Frederic. This location was first fortified by the French, who built Fort St. Frederic in 1734. They destroyed the fort in 1759 as they retreated from the British during the French and Indian War. The British built the much larger Fort Crown Point in 1759 to help control the travel route on Lake Champlain and aid in their conquest of Canada. In 1775 the Green Mountain Boys of Vermont overwhelmed a small garrison of British soldiers and took over the fort near the start of the Revolutionary War. Today this idyllic location along Lake Champlain is also the site of a beautiful new bridge over the lake with walkways that offer views of the historic stone Champlain Memorial Lighthouse and the Crown Point Pier, which are both in the campground area to the south of the fort. The arched bridge is lit at night, making for some great photos against the twilight sky.

Directions: From the main intersection in Crown Point, follow NY 9N/22 north about 3.6 miles. Turn right on Bridge Road (NY 185) at the road sign for the Crown Point Bridge and Vermont. Head east another 3.6 miles to the entrance to the Crown Point State Historic Site on the left, just before the bridge. In another 0.2 mile there is a turnoff on the right that leads to the lighthouse and a campground, as well as a place to park when walking over the bridge. There is a fee for the museum and campground, but none for touring the ruins of the fort, the lighthouse, and the pier by the lighthouse.

French and Indian War reenactment at Fort Ticonderoga

28. Ticonderoga

Ticonderoga is situated on the historic portage route between Lake Champlain and Lake George, which at one time was part of a major water route between New York City and Montreal. This portage had been used for centuries by Native Americans before becoming a very strategic location in battles between the French, Indians, British, and Americans during the 1700s.

The La Chute River, connecting the two lakes, drops 230 feet in about 1.5 miles. There is a beautiful waterfall in Bicentennial Park, near the covered Kissing Bridge, as well as other falls and cascades upstream along the La Chute River Walk. Just east of town is Fort Ticonderoga, which has great photo ops of the beautifully restored fort and traditional gardens. Please note that the fort is private and retains the copyright to any photos taken. Any commercial use of these images must be cleared by the fort.

There are wonderful views of the fort and the southern Lake Champlain basin from the cannon placements on top of Mount Defiance, just south of town. This is a great location to watch the sun rise over the farmland of the Champlain Valley, although you'll have to walk up the road. The gates are open 9–5 daily mid-May through mid-October.

Directions: In Ticonderoga, from the traffic circle at the monument along NY 9N, head east 0.7 mile on Montcalm Street to the parking area at the beginning of Bicentennial Park. The main falls and covered bridge are a short walk downhill on the pathway. To reach the river walk from this parking area, head north on Tower Avenue. The path is on the left just before crossing the bridge over the river. Within a half-mile walk there are a variety of smaller cascades and falls.

Fort Ticonderoga is beyond the park. At 1.2 miles from the traffic circle cross over NY 22. The entrance to the fort is on the right at 1.7

miles. The entrance fee includes access to the fort and gardens ($17.50 adults, mid-May through mid-October). For more information, go to www.fortticonderoga.org.

For the road to Mount Defiance, head east from the traffic circle on Montcalm Street 0.6 mile to the last stoplight before the park. Turn right (south) on Champlain Avenue and head uphill, then bear left at the Y on The Portage. Take the second left, Mount Defiance Street, which narrows and becomes Toll Road. The gate and entrance to the road is at the end of this street.

Pro Tips: One thing I've noticed when photographing around Lake Champlain is the unique quality of light that can occur in calm weather. This is probably related to the valley being bordered by mountains, holding in the moister air over the lake. Colors may be intensified and have a wonderful quality at dawn and dusk. Keep the camera ready for a photo of the elusive "Champ," the Lake Champlain monster.

Cautions: Lake Champlain is 125 miles long, 14 miles across at its widest, and up to 400 feet deep, and the water stays on the cool side. It's a big waterway that can develop some pretty sizable waves in just a gentle wind and huge swells in a real storm. Be well prepared when venturing out on the lake, especially if you're in a small kayak or open canoe, and be aware of any change in the weather that could affect boating conditions.

Diversions: Stay up-to-date on reenactments and other Champlain Valley events at www .lakechamplainregion.com/events.

Sailboats moored along the shore near Valcour Island

Morning light over Lake George from Peggy's Point, Hague

IV. Lake George and the Southeastern Lakes and Mountains

Where: The southeastern corner of the Adirondacks, about an hour north of Albany.

Noted for: Lakes, mountains, and waterfalls.

Best Time: Fall colors peak around the first to third weeks of October, turning first in the higher mountains and last along the Lake George shoreline.

Facilities: In season at the Putnam Pond and Scaroon Manor state campgrounds, the Hague boat launch, Rogers Memorial Park, Lake George Village, the Brant Lake boat launch, and the Schroon Lake town park.

Sleeps and Eats: Along NY 9N from Lake George to Bolton Landing there are lots of lodging and dining locations. Warrensburg and Schroon Lake have numerous options as well. There are a few in the Chestertown area and in Hague, on northern Lake George. Glens Falls, a small city just to the south, has many motels, restaurants, and stores.

General Description: The Lake George area has been a popular tourist destination since the late 1800s. There are several beautiful lakes among the mountains in this region, offering a lot of great photo options, as well as waterfalls and a couple of backcountry hikes.

Directions: Access is from Exits 21 through 29 on the Adirondack Northway (I-87).

Specifically: Bolton Landing, Brant Lake, Chestertown, Hague, Lake George, Loon Lake, Schroon Lake, Warrensburg.

29. Hague

The town of Hague on northern Lake George is situated on the water's edge, with NY 9N following the shoreline for about half a mile. The boat launch in town (free for canoes and kayaks) offers easy access to the state-owned Waltonian Islands just a mile to the north. There are great photo ops from the water-level rocks in the middle of the islands area. In town, there are pretty views over the private beach and dock from the walkway along the road at the Trout House Village Resort. Please respect private property all along the shore.

Peggy's Point, a Lake George Land Conservancy park in the center of town, offers access to the shoreline along the outlet of Hague Brook, with a good view of sunrise light across a large expanse of water. Just south of town is the steamboat landing dock, with broad views over one of the wider sections of the lake. This can be a great location to watch thunderclouds glow in the light of the setting sun. Just west of town is a small park and Hague Brook Falls. The best angle of the falls is from the road—which is rather dangerous with the traffic—or from the stream and pool at the base, which means walking up the rounded stones along the stream to get the shot.

Directions: The town of Hague is at the intersection of NY 9N and 8, which is 9 miles south of the circle in Ticonderoga and 18.5 miles east of Exit 25 on the Northway (I-87). Peggy's Point is just to the east of this intersection, on the north side of Hague Brook. The Trout House Village Resort beach overlook is just north of Peggy's Point along 9N. It's best to walk there from the parking area at Peggy's Point. The Hague boat launch and town beach are along 9N just south of the intersection. The steamboat dock is 0.3 mile south, on Dock Road, which parallels 9N. The parking lot for the falls is on the left (south) side of NY 8, 0.4 mile west of the intersection, just before the hairpin turn.

30. Clay Meadow Area

In addition to a small waterfall and gorge on Northwest Bay Brook, there are also some excellent hiking and canoeing photo destinations here. Just opposite the start of the trail at the Clay Meadow trailhead is a waterfall and small gorge on Northwest Bay Brook. This is not easily visible from the road, but it's only a short walk back to the gorge along the stream from the bridge or along one of the footpaths leading into the woods from the guardrail across from the trailhead. The outlet of the gorge is easiest to get to, while the waterfall itself has rather tricky access, since it's surrounded by the steep rock along the small gorge. It's a nice place to photograph in the soft light of a cloudy day.

The trailhead provides hiking access to the southern Tongue Mountain Range, Northwest Bay, and Montcalm Point. This rugged backcountry is also the northern range of the endangered and protected timber rattlesnake, so be sure to watch your step along the trail.

When hiking from Clay Meadow to the notch between Five Mile Mountain and Fifth Peak, then south along the Tongue Mountain Range, you'll find impressive views beyond the lean-to on Fifth Peak (2.5 miles), as well as great views from French Point Mountain (4.3 miles), from First Peak (5.7 miles), and from many ledges along the trail. Be sure to stop by the state boat dock (7.6 miles) for a dramatic view of the islands and mountains of the Narrows. Montcalm Point is at 8 miles (5.4 miles back to the Clay Meadow trailhead via the scenic shoreline trail).

Just south of the trailhead is the Northwest Bay Brook boat launch. It's a scenic paddle

Pickerelweed and morning light over the Tongue Mountain Range in Northwest Bay, Lake George

Winter sunrise from the steamboat dock at Rogers Memorial Park, Bolton Landing

down the brook into the wetlands of Northwest Bay. Early morning light can be soft and misty, with a variety of wildlife found throughout the wetlands. You can paddle farther along the shoreline out and around Montcalm Point and then access the range trail from the state boat dock, or explore the many state-owned islands in the Narrows. Most of the Tongue Mountain

Range is state land. Please respect the property rights of any private landowners in the area.

Directions: From Exit 24 on the Northway (I-87), head 4.7 miles east on County Route 11 to the T intersection with NY 9N. Turn left (north) on 9N. The sign and parking lot for the boat launch are on the right at 9.1 miles. The parking lot for the trailhead is at 9.3 miles by the small pond, with extra parking in another lot just to the north. The actual trailhead is a short walk back on 9N, and the unmarked footpaths to the falls and gorge are across the street.

31. Rogers Memorial Park

In the summer Bolton Landing is a bustling little village with a wide variety of places to eat and shop. This park is right in town and features a beach and water access, with great views of the Sagamore Resort, mountains, and lake from along the steamboat dock. The sun rises behind Green Island and the Sagamore area. The view can be especially nice before sunrise when there are still some lights on in the buildings. It's also a great place to watch the full moon rise.

Directions: From Exit 24 on the Northway (I-87), head 4.7 miles east on County Route 11 to the T intersection with NY 9N. Turn right and travel another 2 miles south on 9N through Bolton Landing. Rogers Memorial Park Road is on the left beside the library.

32. Million Dollar Beach

One of the most easily accessible views of Lake George is from the pier at the west end of Million Dollar Beach in Lake George Village. This location is great for both sunrise and sunset light, and it's also a great place to photograph the weekly Thursday evening fireworks (in season). At sunrise both the lake and the streets are really quiet. A telephoto lens puts more emphasis on the mountains and water, while a wide-angle lens draws the clouds and shoreline details into the photo. You can always bring along a folding Adirondack chair as a prop.

Directions: From Exit 20 on the Northway (I-87), head east on NY 9N to the light at 0.25 mile. Turn left (north), then at 1.5 miles turn right (east) at the light on Beach Road (County Route 6). There is parking on the right at 1.7 miles across from the steamboat company dock and again at 2.1 miles, where there is a large lot for Million Dollar Beach. The small concrete pier is just to the left (west) of the fenced-off Million Dollar Beach area, which is across from the far parking lot. There is no charge to access the beach areas, but in season there is a fee for parking.

33. Shelving Rock Falls Area

Shelving Rock Brook cascades some 50 feet or more over a sheer rock face and into a pool at the bottom, before flowing through a series of small rocky gorges on its way to a beautiful sandy bay on Lake George. A loop trail passes by the falls (0.3 mile) and follows the brook to its wetland outlet (1.1 miles). From there it heads north to a trail that leads out to the next point (1.5 miles) and then a short distance back up to a parking area (1.9 miles, plus another 0.8 mile back to the car). The falls and gorges are a great place to spend time on a cloudy day, with quick access to the lake in case it clears up enough for a dramatic sunset over

Adirondack chairs set up as props in dawn light along the shore in Lake George Village

Morning fog layers over Brant Lake from the boat launch

the water. This bay is also a popular boating and party destination in the summer, but there are few boats in front of the point at the south end of the bay.

The drive in on the gravel road to the falls passes a trailhead for Buck Mountain (2.3 miles), which has some fabulous views overlooking central Lake George and the mountains, as well as to the High Peaks if it's clear enough. This is a great place to photograph the sunset as long as you are comfortable hiking back out by the light of a headlamp.

Directions: From Exit 20 on the Northway (I-87), head east on NY 9N to the light at 0.25 mile. Turn right (south) on US 9. At 8.9 miles Sly Pond Road becomes Shelving Rock Road by the right-hand turn for Hogtown Road. Continue straight ahead on Shelving Rock Road, and at 9.6 miles turn left by the Hogtown/Lake George Trails System parking area. The Buck Mountain trailhead is on the left at 10.1 miles. At 11.9 miles, at the base of a series of long steep hills, the road crosses a bridge over Shelving Rock Brook, flowing from right to left. A trail to the falls, gorges, and lake is on the left side of the stream. There is a large parking lot just ahead on the left and another at 12.4 miles, where you can access the north end of the trail loop. The trail to the point heads downhill from the right side of this second parking area. There are also other trails in this area, including one that heads farther north along the lakeshore.

34. Brant Lake

This pretty little hamlet has a couple of classic Adirondack views that are especially beautiful in the fall. The old millpond in town has a waterfall at the outlet dam and a fountain in the middle. Both are lit with colored lights in evening twilight. Across the pond from the

Sunrise over Schroon Lake from the pier at Scaroon Manor

dam is a small cobblestone building and a classic white church. A big red maple frames both nicely, especially when the leaves turn in the fall. The boat launch is a short distance away on the main part of the lake, with a view of a turreted summer house on an island and rounded mountains surrounding the lake. Sunrise or sunset can be impressive here, and sunny or cloudy light can be nice in town, especially with fall colors.

Directions: From Exit 25 on the Northway (I-87), head 1.7 miles east on NY 8 to the dam by the millpond. There is parking to the right of the walkway over the dam. It is 2.75 miles to the boat launch, which also has parking.

35. Scaroon Manor

This historic state park and campground along the western shore of beautiful Schroon (pronounced "skroon") Lake features one of the finer morning views on the lake. There's a great view from the pier by the swimming area, as well as from the rocky ledges and shoreline to the north of the pier. A telephoto focal length can help accentuate the distant High Peaks. This is also a great location for sunrise light and clouds. There is a day-use fee from 8 AM until the booth closes, but it's okay to access the park before or after that. If the entrance gates are closed, it's a relatively short walk in to the shore from the gate.

Directions: From the south, take Exit 27 on the Northway (I-87). Head east 0.25 mile and turn right (south) on US 9. Scaroon Manor is on the left at 1.1 miles. From the north, take Exit 28 and turn right on US 9 at 0.25 mile. Head south on 9 through the village of Schroon Lake, reaching the entrance to the park at 8 miles. Drive in past the campground area to the gravel parking area on the left at the T. Walk any path downhill to the water's edge to find the pier.

Pro Tips: With a predominance of hardwoods along many of the waterways in this region, there is an abundance of good locations to view and photograph fall foliage. As nice as the trees can be, remember to look for many different types of reflections on the water. These can show up as colored highlights or intriguing shapes and details. The most intense reflections appear when the water is in shadow and the leaves and other details are sunlit.

Cautions: Lake George and Schroon Lake, like any of the larger bodies of water in the Adirondacks, can change from a mirrorlike surface to raging whitecaps in a matter of minutes in the right conditions. Always keep an eye on the weather and any cloud or wind changes, and have plenty of safety gear and dry bags with you to keep you and your gear safe.

Diversions: The Schroon River parallels the Northway and River Road (first left off Exit 24) for about 3 to 4 miles north of the exit. It has some good photo options along the public fishing sections, especially on a fall afternoon when the sun is shining on the far shore. Please respect private property in this area.

Pack Forest, just off US 9 about 3 miles north of Warrensburg, has a great nature trail with some beautiful old-growth pines. This can be a special place on a quiet day with diffused light conditions.

The Lake George Land Conservancy maintains several preserves around Lake George. Cat Mountain has some really fine views overlooking the Lake George basin—great for sunrise or sunset light. Gull Bay Preserve has a heron rookery, and others protect various unique habitats and views. Check the conservancy's website (www.lglc.org) for maps and additional information.

Shelving Rock Falls

Sunrise light on clouds from Crane Mountain

V. The Southern Adirondacks

Where: The Adirondacks along and south of
NY 8 and west of the Northway (I-87).

Noted for: Rivers, waterfalls, foothill mountains,
and lakes.

Best Time: Fall colors peak around the first
week of October in the higher mountains
near Speculator and around the second and
third weeks in the lower elevations along the
lakes and rivers.

Facilities: In season, and possibly during specific daytime hours, at the Lake Luzerne
beach and Whitewater Park, the Lake
Pleasant beach, state campgrounds, and
the Edinburg boat launch.

Sleeps and Eats: The Lake Luzerne, Northville,
and Speculator areas have the greatest variety
of lodging and dining options in the region.
Just to the south and west, Amsterdam,
Gloversville, and Utica are full-service cities
with many dining, lodging, and shopping
options.

General Description: A mix of rivers, waterfalls, and smaller foothill mountain views make
this a fun area to explore by car, on foot, or in a
canoe.

Directions: From the Adirondack Northway
(I-87), head west from Exits 16 through 25.
From the New York State Thruway (I-90),
head north from Exits 27 through 29, or head
north and east on NY 8 from Exit 31 in Utica.

Specifically: Hadley, Johnsburg, Lake Luzerne, Northville, Piseco Lake, Speculator,
Wells.

36. Crane Mountain

There are views of and from a mountaintop
pond and from the ledges on this small moun-

tain. A short steep climb leads to a trail that loops up and over the rocky ridgeline of the summit and then to Crane Mountain Pond not far below the summit ridge for a 4-mile round-trip. The views from the ridge are mostly to the south and west, so it's tough to get a direct sunrise photo—although the pond can be pretty along the trail near its outlet with sunrise light and clouds reflected in the water.

Not far from the trailhead for Crane Mountain is a canoe access to Garnet Lake. Some of the best views from the lake to Mount Blue and the surrounding mountains are from the northern section of the lake.

Directions: From the intersection of NY 8 and 28 in Wevertown (11 miles west of Exit 25 on the Northway [I-87]), head west on NY 8 for 1.5 miles, then turn left (south) on South Johnsburg Road (County Route 57). At 8.4 miles in Thurman turn right (west) on Garnet Lake Road (County Route 72). At 9.7 miles bear right at the Y, then in 0.1 mile turn right (north) on Ski Hill Road. The gravel road becomes a single lane at about 11 miles and, after a sharp right-hand bend, reaches the parking lot at 11.6 miles. The trail heads about 0.7 mile up to the summit loop. Turn right for the summit or left for the pond. Check the trail map posted at the trail register.

To reach Garnet Lake from NY 8, turn left in Johnsburg on Garnet Lake Road at 1.7 miles from the NY 8/28 intersection (just past South Johnsburg Road). Follow Garnet Lake Road for 6.3 miles. Turn right (south) to reach Garnet Lake in about 1 mile. Follow the left fork along the east side of the lake to the canoe launch site.

37. Lake Luzerne and Hadley

The town of Lake Luzerne offers three photo opportunities within easy walking distance. There's a park with views of an island and the lake, plus several sets of pretty cascades and falls on the outlet stream just across the road in Mill Creek Park. The street side of Mill Creek Park is nicely manicured, with flowers and a gazebo, and the other side has a short footpath that follows high above the stream through some picturesque woods. Just a few hundred feet down Main Street from Mill Creek Park is the lawn around the Chamber of Commerce building, with a nice view of the Hudson River just above Rockwell Falls.

There is a view of the river and falls from the Hadley-Luzerne Bridge, just a short distance farther downriver. The bridge crosses over to Hadley, where a section of the Sacandaga River that's well-known for white-water paddling flows under the historic bow bridge, the only one of its kind in the state. The bow bridge is adjacent to a railroad bridge, which a Saratoga & North Creek Railway tourist train passes over at least twice a day in season. (Check the schedule at www.sncrr.com.) There is an interesting angle on both bridges from the footpath below the south side of the bow bridge. Dean Mountain Whitewater Park, just west of the bridge, provides access for photographing the rapids and boaters on the Sacandaga River, along with a fun angle downstream to both bridges. Water is released for boaters on the river from about 10 to 5 daily through the summer and at other times during the year.

Directions: From Exit 21 on the Northway (I-87), head 9.9 miles south on NY 9N into the village of Lake Luzerne. Wayside Beach on the lake is on the left (east), and Mill Creek Park is along Mill Street, on the right (west). Head down Mill Street and take a left on Main Street. Just past the Adirondack Folk School is the large lawn by the Chamber of Commerce building, where some Adirondack chairs are perched along the edge of the woods by the river. To reach the bow bridge and Dean

Mountain Whitewater Park, drive south down Main Street a few hundred feet more to Rockwell Street on the right. Park anywhere along Rockwell Street to photograph the river from the bridge. Cross the bridge, and at the first full intersection turn left on Old Corinth Road. Follow that a short distance to the bow bridge. On the far (south) side of the bridge, turn right (west) and travel a few hundred feet on unpaved Dean Mountain Road to the parking area for the white-water park on the right.

38. Great Sacandaga Lake and Copeland Covered Bridge

Not far from the shore of Great Sacandaga Lake is a pretty waterfall and small covered bridge over Beecher Creek. Arad Copeland built this bridge in 1879 for his cattle to cross the stream to fields on the other side. It's the only queen post truss bridge in New York. The beautiful 20-foot-high cascading Beecher Creek Falls is just above the bridge. Photographing here can be best on a soft cloudy day or when the hollow is shaded in early morning or late afternoon light.

There are also a number of vantage points over the lake. The eastern arm is more dramatic, with foothill mountains rising from the shore. Just east of the covered bridge is the Saratoga County Park and the Department of Environmental Conservation (DEC) boat launch in Edinburg, a bit farther along is a pull-

Mill Creek cascades in the town park, Lake Luzerne

Beecher Creek Falls from inside the Copeland Covered Bridge, Edinburg

out with a view over the lake, and just beyond that is the road that crosses the Conklingville Dam at the outlet. The predominance of hardwoods makes this a great area for fall foliage photos along the edge of the lake, as well as along the Sacandaga River. The new Batchellerville Bridge (to be completed in 2014), crossing the lake at Edinburg, will have

a wide walkway along its half-mile span. I can imagine some great photos from that bridge overlooking mist and fog lying on the water on a beautiful fall morning.

Directions: From Exit 27 on the New York State Thruway (I-90), head about 25 miles north on NY 30 to the turn across the bridge for Northville (Bridge Street). Head east 0.7 mile and turn right on South Main Street. At 2 miles turn right (south) on Northville Road (County Route 113). At 2.7 miles bear left (east), still following Northville Road. At 5.1 miles continue straight ahead for the Batchellerville Bridge or turn left on North Shore Road (County Route 4) for the covered bridge. At 5.4 miles bear right, staying on North Shore Road. The bridge and falls are on the right at 5.6 miles. The county park and boat launch are farther east at 9.7 miles, a pull-out above the lake is at 15.3 miles, and the turn for the dam is at 20.6 miles. The dam is less than 0.25 mile south on Overlook Road (County Route 8).

39. Tenant Creek Falls

This pretty 50-foot waterfall, also known as Hope Falls, is reached via a 0.9-mile walk along Stony Creek and Tenant Creek. For some distance below the falls, Tenant Creek is as pretty as an Adirondack stream can be. This section is especially nice when the beech trees along the opposite shore turn golden in the fall. If you want to hike farther, there are two more waterfalls about a mile upstream. The access is open to the public but is on private land. Please remain on the trail and respect the privacy of the landowners.

Directions: From the intersection of NY 30 and Bridge Street just west of Northville, head north 6.6 miles on 30 to Creek Road in Hope. Turn right (east) and travel 2.9 miles, then turn left (north) on Hope Falls Road (County Route

A rather long exposure of the water and foliage on Tenant Creek below the falls

7). Travel 7.8 miles along Stony Creek to a small parking lot and trail register. From here it's 0.2 mile to a trail on the right, which is just before a substantial snowmobile bridge over the creek. Follow this trail east along Tenant Creek to the falls.

40. Auger Falls

The 40-foot drop at the falls is only a small part of this Sacandaga River experience. The falls, and the steep-sided flume and cascades below it, can be accessed by a 0.4-mile walk. The 1.2-mile loop hike that goes along the river above the falls offers many additional photo opportunities. The forest here has a very primeval feel and has many photo possibilities in the soft light of a cloudy day. In low water the exposed potholes show how Auger Falls got its name.

Directions: From the junction of NY 8 and 30 a couple of miles north of Wells, head north on 30 for 1.7 miles to the small, easily missed dirt road on the right (east) side of the road. For the short route to the falls, turn right again in about 50 feet on the dirt road that parallels NY 30. Go about 0.1 mile to the small parking area and trailhead. If you're doing the loop, after you turn off 30 continue straight ahead into the gravel parking area. Park at the far end of the lot. Walk down the gravel road on the right to the lower gravel area. At the east end, a footpath cuts off to the right across a small wet area and then heads slightly uphill. This unmarked trail goes south along the river and intersects the marked trail at the top of the hill just past Auger Falls.

41. Austin Falls

You can drive right to the falls—unless your car has a low-slung suspension system. The drop at the end of the falls is only about 10 feet, but the few hundred feet of long sloping cascades above the drop, and the rapids and pools below, offer lots of options for shooting. Several

Rocks and ferns along the Sacandaga River just above Auger Falls

small potholes in the sloped rocks along the flowing water are of interest, too.

Directions: From the intersection of NY 8 and 30 a couple of miles north of Wells, drive 6.6 miles north and turn right on Old NY 30. The road soon crosses the Sacandaga River and follows the east side of the river. This road is not maintained and has many frost heaves. It's 2.7 miles to the cascades and falls.

42. Speculator

Speculator's town park, with flower beds and Adirondack-style benches, and its public beach are situated at the east end of Lake Pleasant. Although the summer sun sets over the swimming area, rather than across the length of the lake, there are still a lot of options for shooting at sunset when clouds span the sky above the lake. In the morning the sun is behind you, highlighting any mist on the water.

Just across the road from the park, the lake's outlet may be shrouded in morning mist, and there's some great canoeing and photo options to the east along the river, as well as in Kunjamuk Bay a couple of miles to the east. Kunjamuk Bay can also be accessed from a parking area along NY 30/8 just east of Speculator. It's pretty in both morning mist and evening's magic hour light. Another location with good shooting options along the road is the outlet of Sacandaga Lake, a few miles west of the center of town. Just north of town is Whiskey Brook Falls, a small but easily accessed and attractive waterfall about two hundred feet from the road. It's a great diversion on a cloudy day that's easy to access.

Directions: From the main intersection in Speculator, where NY 8 heads west and NY 30 heads north, travel 0.5 mile south on NY 8/30 to the beach and park. Parking is available in the lot just before the beach on the left or along the main road. The Kunjamuk Bay access

along NY 8/30 is 1.8 miles south of the intersection in town. Pull into the gravel parking lot just south of the paved one, then take the short path down to the water's edge.

The outlet of Sacandaga Lake is 3 miles west of town along NY 8. A few canoes or kayaks passing by can add some nice color to your shots. Whiskey Brook Falls is 3.7 miles north of town on the east side of NY 30, at the edge of a cleared area along the road. The falls are visible in the woods beyond the edge of the clearing. Park along the highway at both of these locations.

43. Piseco Lake

Three state campgrounds offering some open sandy shorelines, as well as a short climb to Echo Cliff overlooking the lake and surrounding foothill mountains, provide a number of shooting options around the Piseco Lake area. All of these locations are on the western shore, so photo ops are best at sunrise or in evening light when the sun is going down behind you. While my preferences are Poplar Point and Point Comfort state campgrounds, there are some good shoreline options at Little Sand Point state campground as well. The view from Echo Cliff is to the south and east. There's a 180-degree panoramic view over the surrounding landscape from the open ledges at the end of the steep 0.8-mile trail.

Directions: From the intersection of NY 8 and 30 in Speculator, head west on 8 for 8.9 miles and turn right (north) on Old Piseco Road (County Route 24). Follow this road around to the west side of the lake. Poplar Point is at about 3.8 miles, Little Sand Point is at 4.9 miles, Panther Mountain/Echo Cliff trailhead parking is at 5.3 miles, and Point Comfort is at 6.8 miles. Continue past Point Comfort to reach NY 8 at 8 miles. Day-use fees may apply for accessing the shoreline when the campgrounds are open.

Mist at dawn over Kunjamuk Bay near Speculator

Sunrise at Point Comfort state campground, Piseco Lake

Pro Tips: To get a softer milky or misty effect when photographing the waterfalls in this region, add a neutral density filter or a polarizing filter to cut down on the light. Drop the ISO down to the lowest setting (50 or 100 ISO, or L (low) 1.0). Use aperture priority, and set the aperture to its smallest setting.

Most polarizers cut down the amount of light by 2 stops, which will drop the shutter speed enough to blur the water nicely even on a sunny day. Adjustable or fixed neutral density filters cut the light from 2 to as many as 10 stops. If you're using a 10-stop neutral density filter, focus first, then add the filter and adjust the aperture, shutter, and ISO as needed. For exposures longer than 30 seconds, use manual mode, adjust the shutter setting to bulb, and use a remote release with locking capability.

Be sure to use a viewfinder cover, or cover the viewfinder with a handkerchief or strap, when you're using a neutral density filter. If the viewfinder is left uncovered, the light meter will read the light coming through it, thus creating a darker than expected exposure.

Cautions: Use extra care on the sloped rocks around the waterfalls. With even just a bit of condensation on a humid day, or in misty or rainy conditions, many of these rocks can be as slippery as wet ice.

Diversions: If the morning sky looks promising for sunrise colors, take a quick run to the beach at the Luzerne state campground on NY 9N just a couple of miles east of the town of Lake Luzerne. Turn right at the T just past the tollbooth on the entrance road, then continue several hundred feet to the large parking lot. There's a short paved path to the beach. Fourth Lake typically has wonderful reflections on a calm morning.

Sunset over the Moose River from the Green Bridge, Thendara

VI. Old Forge Area and the Fulton Chain of Lakes

General Description: This popular area is part of a historic water route that extends across the Fulton Chain of Lakes from Old Forge to Inlet, Raquette Lake, the Raquette River, Indian Lake, and finally the Saranac Lakes in the north-central Adirondacks. There are many lakes, ponds, streams, and cascades throughout this region.

Directions: This area lies along NY 28, which is accessed from NY 12 heading north from Utica on the west, or from NY 30 and 28 in Blue Mountain Lake.

Specifically: Eagle Bay, Inlet, Old Forge, Raquette Lake, Thendara.

44. Moose River

The Moose River is rather prominent in this area, flowing west from the wilderness ponds north of Inlet into the Black River a few miles west of the Adirondack Park. The Moose River roughly parallels NY 28 for a number of miles west of Old Forge, with various places to stop and photograph. One spot I like in particular is several miles west of Thendara, where 28 meets up with Scusa Road. The river flows around a bend and through a stretch of boulders. Since it is flowing in a westerly direction, there are magic hour light options in both morning and evening.

About a mile farther south and west along 28, a fairly level half-mile trail leads from a parking area down to the Moose River. The first section of the river you reach flows south, while the section up by the railroad bridge flows east. Check the Adirondack Scenic Railroad schedule for the Thendara–Otter Lake

> **Where:** The west-central Adirondacks.
> **Noted for:** Lakes, foothill mountains, streams, and rivers.
> **Best Time:** Fall colors tend to peak around the end of September and the first week of October.
> **Facilities:** In season at Arrowhead Park in Inlet and at Camp Sagamore when open.
> **Sleeps and Eats:** The Old Forge/Thendara area has the greatest variety of lodging and meal options. There are also a number of places to dine and stay in the Eagle Bay/Inlet area.

schedule (www.adirondackrr.com) if you'd like to try getting a photo of the train crossing the bridge over this wild section of the river. Lots of hardwoods line the river here, which is great for softly lit fall foliage photos with long exposures of the water flowing over and around the rocks. The south-flowing section is perfect for fall colors reflected across the flowing water in midafternoon, when the far shore is highlighted by the sun and the river is in shadow from the trees on the western shore.

Directions: Scusa Road is off NY 28. The east entrance is 5.1 miles west of the substantial bridge over the Moose River between Old Forge and Thendara. The west entrance is 0.5 mile farther, or about 21 miles east of NY 12 near Forestport. Follow the road from either entrance until you see the river. The boulders are at the east end of the section, where the river is beside the road. Park safely along the road and find the footpath to the water near where the road starts to go uphill.

The Moose River trail is 6.8 miles west of

the Old Forge–Thendara bridge. This un-marked trail heads east and north through the woods. Bear left at the first cutoff, then cross over the railroad tracks and follow the small footpath north to various sections of rocky rapids until you reach the railroad bridge.

45. Old Forge and Thendara

There are two bridges just a short distance apart that offer different photo ops over and along the Moose River. The Old Forge–Thendara bridge is on NY 28 and has a good angle for photographing summer sunset light with clouds reflecting in the quiet waters by the bridge. The Green Bridge also has a level, 1-mile trail along a quiet section of the river that offers nice angles on sunrise and sunset light and reflections. You may see waterfowl, deer, and other wildlife in this area, as well as vibrant fall colors in the trees along the shore by the bridge.

Directions: The Old Forge–Thendara bridge is on NY 28 over the Moose River. Access the Green Bridge in Thendara by taking NY 28 west from the Old Forge–Thendara bridge. At 0.8 mile bear left on Forge Street, leaving 28. At 0.9 mile turn left on Beech Street. After the sharp left bend at 1.2 miles, turn right on Green Bridge Road at 1.25 miles. There is a parking area at 1.4 miles, on the south side of the bridge. The trail along the river heads west from the parking area, with different vantage points over the quiet backwater behind a dam.

Reflections and ice on the Moose River

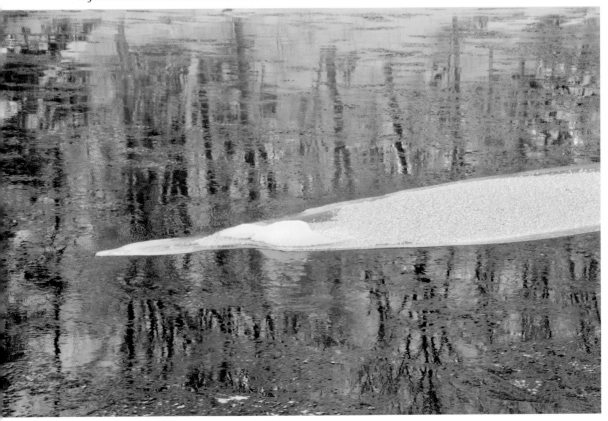

Afternoon light over Fourth Lake from Bald Mountain

46. Bald Mountain

The views from the open rock ledges and fire tower on top of Bald Mountain provide the best views of the lakes in the Old Forge/Inlet area. The 1-mile trail to the summit has less than 400 feet of elevation gain, so it's an easy climb compared to many other mountain trails in the park. There are several open ledges on the way to the summit. The view is mostly to the east and south, making it a great location to photograph sunrise over morning mist in the valleys or the effects of afternoon magic hour light on the landscape. There are great views from the open ledges on the summit, and even broader views over the tall pines from the restored fire tower.

Directions: From the Old Forge Hardware intersection in the center of Old Forge, head east on NY 28 for 4.8 miles, then turn left on Rondaxe Road (County Route 93) at the sign for Bald Mountain. The parking lot is on the left (west) side of the road, 0.2 mile from NY 28.

47. Moss Lake

Moss Lake is a pretty lake with a small island close to the center. The long sandy beach area, less than a quarter mile from the parking lot, has a view of the island and the mountain on the opposite side of the lake. Moss Lake is a great place to explore and photograph from a canoe. You can also access different vantage points from the 2.5-mile trail that circles the lake.

Directions: From NY 28 head north on Big Moose Road in Eagle Bay, just west of Inlet. The main parking lot for Moss Lake is at 2.1

Morning light over rising fog at Moss Lake

miles, on the left (west) side of the road. Follow the trail across the loop trail for the shortest route to the lakeshore.

48. Rocky Mountain and Black Bear Mountain

Just west of Inlet is the trailhead for two popular mountain climbs in the area. It's a half-mile hike to the open ledges at the summit of Rocky Mountain. There are 180-degree views from the southeast to the west overlooking the Eagle Bay/Fourth Lake/Inlet area. The winter sun sets almost directly over the lakes, while the summer sun sets much farther north.

Black Bear Mountain is a 4.1-mile hike to a rocky ridgeline with views of Blue Mountain to the east and the thin ribbon of Seventh Lake, set among the nearby foothill mountains, to the south. This view can be spectacular at sunrise with a thin layer of mist over the wetlands and trees in the valley and the sun rising behind Blue Mountain in the distance.

Directions: The trailhead for both mountains is along NY 28, 1.1 miles east of the intersection of Big Moose Road and 28 in Eagle Bay. There are a couple of junctions along the trail to Black Bear Mountain. At the first trail junction, follow the shorter blue trail (4.1 miles total) or the longer yellow trail (5.2 miles) to the summit.

49. Inlet

Arrowhead Park is a town park along the paddling route from Fourth Lake to Fifth Lake.

Sunrise behind Blue Mountain from the summit of Black Bear Mountain

Lights along the shoreline of Fourth Lake from Arrowhead Park, Inlet

With beautiful views west over Fourth Lake, this is a great location for sunset light and clouds. Lights along the shoreline can enhance an evening twilight shoot. There is also a good view from the state boat launch dock area just west of Arrowhead Park.

Directions: The parking area for Arrowhead Park is in the center of Inlet, on the west side of the bend in NY 28 where most of the stores are located, by the information center. Enter the park at the far end of the parking lot. The Department of Environmental Conservation (DEC) boat launch is about 0.5 mile west of Arrowhead Park on the south side of the road. It's rather long and narrow and easily missed.

50. Raquette Lake

The Raquette Lake area has three easy access points where you can photograph right along the road. While these locations can be nice at any time of the day with the right clouds and light, they are especially lovely when there is some broken fog and mist to catch the morning light, adding an air of mystery to the larches, wetlands, and meandering and open waters. Each spot has a different character. Since they're rather close to one another, it's good to scout them first to decide what light and time of day you'd like for each. Exploring any of these locations by canoe or kayak gives you additional photo options. A paddle to the end of South Inlet brings you to a small waterfall where the stream from Sagamore Lake flows into Raquette Lake, plus the opportunity to view wildlife along the way. Death Falls, a 70-foot cascade, is a just a quarter-mile walk from the road. With a good flow of water, it is much prettier than its name might suggest. In dry weather, though, it is barely a trickle.

Directions: At the west end of Raquette Lake, from the intersection of NY 28, Sagamore

Sunrise light on clouds over Otter Bay from along NY 28

Road, and CR 2, head north 0.2 mile on CR 2 toward Raquette Lake village and park along the road near the bridge. The sun rises over the wetland and lake, and there can be good light over the Brown Tract Flow on the opposite side of the road as well. At 0.6 mile east of the intersection of NY 28, Sagamore Road, and CR 2, 28 meets the shoreline of Raquette Lake along Otter Bay in a bend in the road. Park along the road just east of this bend. The sun rises over the bay, with Blue Mountain off in the distance. At 2.5 miles east of the main intersection, there's a bridge and view over South Inlet on the right (south) side of NY 28, with Raquette Lake on the north side. At 3.5 miles, park along 28, near the blocked-off access road on the right (south) side, to access Death Falls.

51. Great Camp Sagamore

Sagamore is one of the finest examples of a traditional rustic Adirondack great camp. It was built by the developer William West Durant in the late 1800s and then purchased in 1901 by Alfred Vanderbilt. The Vanderbilt family used this camp until the 1950s. Today it's a designated national historic landmark that is being preserved by the Sagamore Institute. Overnight lodging is available in season, and workshops and tours are offered in the summer and fall. Twenty-seven buildings have been preserved, including the renowned main lodge, a spacious dining hall, the beautiful rustic boathouse, the bowling alley, the root cellar, guesthouses, and workers' quarters and barns. Check out www.greatcampsagamore.org for more information and tour schedules.

Directions: At the west end of Raquette Lake, from the intersection of NY 28, Sagamore Road, and CR 2, head south 3.6 miles on unpaved Sagamore Road to the Great Sagamore Camp parking lot.

Pro Tips: On warm summer mornings before and just after sunrise, each receding "layer" of the landscape often has a light misty edge, making for some great photos of the otherwise rather flat and soft scenery. The same effect can be seen in successive layers of mountains from an open mountaintop or ledge, or along the edge of a lake or field. Working with telephoto focal lengths helps isolate the layers from more distracting details in the scene. The colors of the mist change with those in the sky. Sunrise light is nice and warm. As the sun rises higher in the sky, the light cools off to a bluer tone.

Cautions: Although the lakes in this region aren't too large, they can still be quite dangerous in storms and strong winds. Keep an eye on weather reports—and the sky—before venturing out in a canoe or kayak. This area receives a lot of snow throughout the winter. Be sure to use snowshoes or skis for any backcountry travel.

Diversions: Just east of Inlet is the western access to the Moose River Plains Wild Forest, an expansive area with unpaved road access that stretches to just west of Indian Lake. There is a state campground at Limekiln Lake, many beautiful ponds that can be accessed by short drives and trails from the main road, and opportunities for fishing, mountain biking, and more. For more information, go to www.dec.ny .gov/lands/53596.html.

Rustic architecture at Great Camp Sagamore

Canoeing at sunset on Lake Lila

VII. Northwestern Lakes and Waters

Where: The northwestern Adirondacks, north of Indian Lake and west of Lake Placid.

Noted for: Lakes, ponds, bogs, waterways, and waterfalls.

Best Time: Fall colors peak from late September to the first week of October.

Facilities: In season at Meacham Lake campground and at Paul Smith's College Visitor Interpretive Center, but none at other parking areas.

Sleeps and Eats: Saranac Lake has many options for both lodging and dining, with additional choices in the Tupper Lake area.

General Description: The northwestern Adirondack plateau has numerous lakes and ponds feeding the Raquette and Grasse Rivers, which drop west into the St. Lawrence Valley with many rapids, cascades, and waterfalls. The Saranac River flows east through the historic village of Saranac Lake on its way to the northern Champlain Valley.

Directions: From the south follow NY 30 from Indian Lake. From the west travel NY 3 from I-81 and Watertown. From Potsdam use NY 56 to NY 3. From the north take NY 30. From Plattsburgh and the northeast use NY 3. From Lake Placid travel west on NY 86.

Specifically: Cranberry Lake, Paul Smiths, St. Regis Falls, Saranac Lake, Tupper Lake.

52. Lake Lila Region

Lake Lila is one of the prettiest state-owned lakes I've had the opportunity to explore. It's a long drive on an unpaved road plus a half-mile portage to get a canoe to the shore, but it's well worth the effort. The tall pines towering over the bays, peninsulas, and islands add a lot of character to photos. A short hike to the open ledges on Frederica Mountain, at the west end of the lake, leads to great views east over the lake and south over the surrounding wilderness.

Along the way to Lake Lila stop by Round Lake and Little Tupper Lake. Little Tupper Lake has an open view along the road looking west, and there are a variety of photo ops on Round Lake within a short distance of the canoe access. In addition to a number of large rocky areas in the water a short distance up the Round Lake inlet, there's an island, a small sandy beach on the east side, and a cascade not far from the lake's outlet.

Directions: Circle Road (County Route 10A) meets NY 30 in two locations, about 6.5 miles north of the bridge in Indian Lake and again 3.6 miles north of that, which is about 11 miles south of downtown Tupper Lake. Follow Circle Road from either end about 3 miles to the intersection with Sabattis Road, by the open shoreline of Little Tupper Lake. Turn west on Sabattis Road. The first bridge, at 0.2 mile, crosses over the inlet to Round Lake. At 1.3 miles is the main Department of Environmental Conservation (DEC) access for Little Tupper Lake. The road soon becomes dirt. At 4.5 miles, turn left at the sign for Lake Lila and drive to the parking lot at about 10.2 miles. It's a half-mile walk to the sandy eastern shore of the lake. A 4.4-mile trail to Frederica Mountain also starts here. A 1.6-mile trail to Frederica Mountain starts at the clearing on the west side of Lake Lila.

53. Tupper Lake

Bog River Falls, at the south end of Tupper Lake, is a great place to photograph moving and cascading water. There is always a good flow, and it's a fairly open area, so there are options for all types of lighting. There is access to both sides of the twin sloping falls and also interesting composition options around the rapids that rush into the lake from under the bridge. Some sections are tougher to access than others, but they're all just off the road. Morning light, with mist rising off the water on a cool summer or fall day, adds a great touch.

Only 1.5 miles south of the turnoff to Bog River Falls is a 1-mile hike to the rocky summit of Coney Mountain. There are a number of vantage points from the summit ledges, with at least one view east to the High Peaks.

If you go north on NY 30 along Tupper Lake, the view west into Rock Island Bay has different photo opportunities throughout the day. As you continue north, soon after the speed limit goes down, there is a state boat launch on the west side of the highway, with a wide-open vantage point over the lake. Just east of the town of Tupper Lake, the parking area along the causeway is a great stop, with Big Simon Pond and some distant peaks to the east and the wetlands and waters of Tupper Lake to the west. This can be a good location to see wildlife, too. In town there is a park that is great for sunsets, with wide-open views west over the broad expanse of Raquette Pond.

Directions: At the intersection of NY 30 and 421 about 9 miles south of Tupper Lake, turn west on 421 by the DEC sign for Horseshoe Lake. Parking for Bog River Falls is just past the bridge, 0.75 mile from NY 30. To reach the trailhead for Coney Mountain from the intersection of NY 30 and 421, drive south on 30 for 1.6 miles. Parking is on the right (west) side of the highway, and the trailhead is on the left (east) side, just before the parking area. Parking for Rock Island Bay is on NY 30, 1.8 miles north of its intersection with 421. The state boat launch is on the left (west) side of 30 at 6 miles, and the pullout along the causeway is at 7 miles. This pullout is about 2 miles from the town park, which is on the west side of NY 3,

Sunlight over Rock Island Bay

Hornbeck canoe in late afternoon light on Lower Saranac Lake

0.3 mile west of the intersection of NY 3 and 30 in downtown Tupper Lake. There is a walkway along the waterfront.

54. Saranac Lakes

The abundance of lakes and ponds in this region opens up many options for canoeing to photo locations. Upper, Middle, and Lower Saranac Lakes are part of the chain of lakes and rivers that once formed a major transportation network across the Adirondacks. While a good portion of the shoreline of Upper Saranac Lake is privately owned, all of Middle Saranac Lake and much of Lower Saranac Lake are surrounded by state-owned land.

Both Middle and Lower Saranac Lakes have state boat launches for putting in a canoe or kayak. Middle Saranac Lake has a few islands, a long sandy beach along the eastern shore, and a rather gentle shoreline with tall pines, all surrounded by some low foothill mountains. Lower Saranac Lake has many rocky islands. Some, such as The Rock and Bluff Island, have views to higher mountains in the south. There are many photo options, including the roadside view to the mountains over Second Pond from the NY 3 bridge by the state boat launch for Lower Saranac Lake.

It's a steep 2.7-mile climb to the top of Ampersand Mountain, but the views from the open summit are well worth the effort. Ampersand has a rather unique perspective, overlooking the lakes region to the north and west and the High Peaks to the south and east.

Directions: For access to Lower Saranac Lake, from the intersection of Main Street and NY 3 in Saranac Lake, head west on NY 3 for 4 miles to the Second Pond state boat launch on the left (south) side of the highway. Continue west to trailhead parking for Ampersand Mountain on the right (north) side at 8.1 miles and to the South Inlet access to Middle Saranac Lake on the left (south) side at 9.8 miles. It's about a half-mile paddle along the inlet to the main part of the lake.

55. Saranac Lake Village

This historic village still has many of the original "cure cottages" that were home to thousands who came to be cured of tuberculosis over the years. The Church Street historic district showcases a number of the cottages, with their customary open-air porches, as well as three vintage churches and an old medical laboratory. Newer in town is the one-of-a-kind Adirondack Carousel in William Morris Memorial Park, featuring locally crafted hand-carved animals that are all indigenous to the Adirondacks.

Everyone looks forward to the annual Saranac Lake Winter Carnival, the longest-running event of its kind in the eastern United States. Each year a new ice palace is built, and it is lit at night with a variety of colored lights. The fireworks over the palace at the opening and closing ceremonies provide some great photo opportunities.

The summit of Mount Baker has a few large ledges with views over the town and lakes to the west and the High Peaks to the south and east. It's an 800-foot climb up the 1-mile trail to the top from the shore of Moody Pond. The best views are found by exploring the ledges. This is a great place for photographing twilight over the village and lakes—as long as you have a headlamp to light the way back down.

Not far north of the village NY 86 offers classic roadside views across open fields to Whiteface Mountain and other High Peaks in

Carved animal detail on the Adirondack Carousel in Saranac Lake

the distance. There are good views from near the intersection of NY 86 and 186 at Donnelly's Corner, plus others a bit farther north—just south of the Harrietstown cemetery. Please respect any Private Property signs. This view is best with enough clarity and some clouds to add mood. The sun and full moon rise behind the Whiteface Mountain ridgeline, and the setting sun highlights the whole range and valley.

Directions: NY 3 and 86 follow Church Street through Saranac Lake. The historic district extends from the park along Lake Flower, where the ice palace is built each February, to Bloomingdale Road. The carousel is at the corner of Bloomingdale and Church Streets on the north side of Bloomingdale, just opposite the Stewart's. Continue along 86 about 4.6 miles to the intersection with NY 186 at Donnelly's Corner, then 1.6 miles farther to the views near the cemetery. For Baker Mountain, head northeast on Main Street to the T on Pine Street. Turn right (east), then from its intersection with Church Street, turn left on East Pine Street. Follow East Pine Street to the sharp bend at the northeast corner of Moody Pond, and park along the road just around the bend.

56. Paul Smiths

The trail system at Paul Smith's College Visitor Interpretive Center (VIC) traverses some of the most ecologically diverse habitats in the Adirondack Park and offers opportunities for photographing bog habitat and wild orchids, as well as birds and other wildlife. The well-maintained trails include a boardwalk over a section of a sphagnum bog, plus nice views over waterways on the preserve. The four trails closest to the parking for the interpretive center offer some of the greatest diversity. The VIC also maintains a butterfly house through the summer months. For more information, go to www.adirondackvic.org.

St. Regis Pond in the St. Regis Canoe Area

Not far from the VIC is the trailhead for the 3.4-mile footpath to St. Regis Mountain, with beautiful views to the east, south, and west from the open rock at the 2,874-foot summit. The historic fire tower at the top, which will soon be restored, was erected in 1918 and is one of only two dozen remaining in the park. The tower provides a 360-degree view of the northern Adirondack landscape. This is a great location to photograph a sunrise, especially when the valleys are draped with layers of mist and fog.

This is some of the finest wilderness canoe country in the Adirondacks, with access to the St. Regis Canoe Area nearby. While the canoe area is in the backcountry, there are three beautiful ponds near the VIC right next to the main roads. Church Pond is just south of the VIC entrance. The hardwoods surrounding this pretty little pond can be quite spectacular during peak fall colors. Just north of the VIC entrance are Barnum Pond, on the west side of NY 30, and Mountain Pond, on the east side of 30. Each of these has a completely different character and view, with Barnum Pond set in a boreal habitat and Mountain Pond having a more mountainous, hardwood habitat.

Directions: From the intersection of NY 30 and 86 by Paul Smith's College, head east on Easy Street (NY 86) 0.2 mile to the access landing on Church Pond. From the intersection travel 0.9 mile north on 30 to the entrance to the VIC. At 1.75 miles you can park along the road by Barnum Pond. At 2.6 miles unpaved Mountain Pond Road cuts off to the right (east) and follows the pond's shore for about 1 mile. For St. Regis Mountain, head briefly north on 30 from its intersection with 86, then turn left (west) on Keese Mills Road. At 2.4 miles turn left (south) on a gravel road and travel another 0.5 mile to the trailhead to the right of the gate.

57. Meacham Lake Area

I saw my first bald eagle at Meacham Lake many years ago, and visitors to the lake usually aren't disappointed today either. While eagles are seen on occasion throughout the Adirondacks, they are pretty common along many of the lakes and ponds in this vicinity. Loons are also regaining their original range throughout the Adirondacks and can be seen and heard on most lakes here today.

Clear Pond is a pretty body of water beside the entrance to the state campground. Meacham Lake is a larger lake that's about 2 miles long and 1 mile wide. There are nice views of the surrounding mountains to the east from the western shoreline, and there are additional vantage points around the lake that can be accessed by canoe. A little mist in the morning adds a mystical effect. The north end of the lake can be accessed from the campground boat launch or beach (day-use fee in season), or from the main road via canoe on the outlet at the south end of the lake. The Osgood River flows into the south end of the lake through some boggy, boreal growth that's sprinkled with stunted larch and spruce trees, along with pitcher plants and sundews.

Directions: From the intersection of NY 30 and 86 by Paul Smith's College, head north on 30 to the outlet of Meacham Lake at 9.2 miles, shortly after passing Santa Clara Road (NY 458) on the left. The state campground access and Clear Pond are on the right at 11.7 miles.

58. Debar Pond

Tall mountains flanking the south end of the pond, which is oriented north-south, makes this a good location for shooting in both morning and evening magic hour light. There is minimal elevation obstruction on the north end of the pond, so the foreground holds light

Debar Mountain from Clear Pond

Looking south over Debar Pond

just about as long as the mountaintops. It's a 0.3-mile walk from the parking area to the water, easy enough to portage a canoe or kayak so you can explore more of this pretty pond.

Directions: About 5.6 miles north of the Meacham Lake campground entrance, turn right (east) on County Route 26 (Old NY 99). It's about 10 miles to the unpaved access road, which is on the right (south) 0.16 mile after the sharp right-hand turn at the sign for Loon Lake. Drive past the Private sign 0.8 mile from the main road to the parking area. The road beyond the gate leads to Debar Pond Lodge, a log great camp, and the trail leads to the shoreline east of the camp.

Pro Tips: All light is good light! Digital cameras make it easier to capture image information in all lighting conditions. While magic hour light will still be best in many landscape situations, every type of light highlights subjects in a different way. My general rule of thumb is, when it's bright and sunny, I work out in the open, and when cloudy conditions create more diffused light, I work with details in the forests or along the streams and waterways. This is just a guideline, though, as I've shot both open and closed in landscapes in many different lighting conditions.

Most important is to pay attention to little features that catch your eye. While these details may not be strong enough to become a photo on their own, they often work well as part of a broader composition and help draw the eye in and around a photograph. I find it's the eye-catching details that in many cases add the most energy to an image and help make every image unique.

Cautions: The Saranac Lakes are quite exposed to high winds and storms. As with other large bodies of water in the region, use caution regarding the weather.

Diversions: Some other locations in this region to consider include the nature trails at the Wild Center in Tupper Lake, which wander through various woodland habitats and along the Raquette River. Be sure to check out the treetop trail for some unique photo ops. If you enjoy photographing waterfalls, you'll be in heaven viewing the rapids and waterfalls of the Grasse River as it parallels Tooley Pond Road northwest of Cranberry Lake. Within less than 20 miles along the road, there's access to numerous waterfalls and rapids.

West of the Meacham Lake area and south of St. Regis Falls, the 1-mile hike up Azure Mountain leads to good views south over the Adirondack landscape from the open ledges on top of the summit cliffs, with additional views from the restored fire tower. This is also a peregrine falcon nesting area. Not far from the Azure Mountain trailhead, the Santa Clara Flow on the St. Regis River has photo ops of the extensive wetlands along the river. Everton Falls and a beautiful flow on the East Branch of the St. Regis River are farther north and several miles east of St. Regis Falls.

Fog and mountain layers from St. Regis Mountain

Chazy Lake from Lyon Mountain

VIII. Northeastern Mountains and Rivers

Where: The northern Adirondacks, east of NY 30, north of Lake Placid, and west of Plattsburgh and the Northway (I-87).
Noted for: Lakes, rivers, mountains, and bogs.
Best Time: Fall colors peak around the first week of October.
Facilities: At Taylor Pond state campground and the canoe access on Franklin Falls Pond, but none at any other parking areas.
Sleeps and Eats: There are a few bed & breakfasts and diners scattered among the towns, but the greatest variety of lodging and dining can be found on the periphery, in Plattsburgh, Saranac Lake, and Lake Placid.

General Description: This is less traveled country, with many foothill mountains and a few larger ones that offer views over the lakes and rivers in the area. The Saranac River flows from the southwest part of this region to Plattsburgh and Lake Champlain. Two impoundments on the river to the east of Bloomingdale have created some beautiful lakes and flows, with several lovely viewpoints.

Directions: Access from the east is by Exits 30, 31, 34, and 37 on the Adirondack Northway (I-87). Access routes from the west and south are NY 3, 86, and 9N.

Specifically: Bloomingdale, Franklin Falls Pond, Lyon Mountain, Redford, Saranac River, Union Falls Pond.

59. Lyon Mountain

Lyon Mountain, accessible by a 3.5-mile trail, is the highest mountain in the northern Adirondacks. At 3,830 feet, it's just shy of having

Evening clouds over Lyon Mountain and Chazy Lake

4,000-foot High Peak status. It was recently added to the New York State Forest Preserve through a transaction aided by the Nature Conservancy. The summit fire tower provides a full 360-degree view that ranges from the wild High Peaks to the south to Montreal's skyscrapers to the north. There are also open ledges with panoramic views to the east over Chazy Lake and the northern Adirondack hills, with Lake Champlain and Vermont's Green Mountains on the horizon.

Directions: Take NY 374 west from Plattsburgh. Just west of Chazy Lake, turn left (south) on Chazy Lake Road and go 1.75 miles to the Department of Environmental Conservation (DEC) sign for Chazy Highlands and the Lyon Mountain trailhead. It's just under 1 mile to the parking lot by the start of the trail.

60. Chazy Lake

Although most of the Chazy Lake shoreline is privately owned, there are two public access points. The town beach area along NY 374 has a grand view down the lake to Lyon Mountain, and the pump house access has a panoramic view west across the lake. Lyon Mountain is highlighted best in morning light from the town beach. The westerly view from the pump house access is great for photographing sunsets across a mile-wide expanse of water that's flanked by Lyon Mountain to the south and Ellenburg Mountain to the north.

Directions: From the intersection of NY 374 (Cook Street) and Emmons Street in Dannemora, it's 4 miles to the turnoff on the left (south) for Wilfred King Road. Follow this road 2.25 miles to the pump house access. The

Dannemora town beach is on the south side of NY 374, 6.1 miles from the intersection in Dannemora.

61. Bloomingdale

The view of Whiteface Mountain from Norman Ridge Road, over an open field and old weathered barn, is an iconic Adirondack image. Because of the angle of view, the barn is lit from behind in the morning and lit either in front or slightly on the side in the late afternoon. Of course, this isn't the only angle for photographing the barn and mountain background. There are many different options throughout the day and night, perhaps working with the stars or rising moon. There's another barn on the west side of the road with a stunning backdrop of mountain peaks. Remember, these fields are private property; please respect the owners' rights.

Moose Pond is a wild pond on state land just east of Bloomingdale. Access is by an unpaved road to the rustic boat launch site. The view from the boat launch is nice, but about halfway down the roughly mile-long pond the panoramic view east across the water to Whiteface and McKenzie Mountains is spectacular. A few rocky shoreline sections can be easily reached by canoe or by hiking the trail along the western shore. In late spring and midsummer the sun rises to the north of Whiteface and Esther Mountains, but in fall and winter the sun rises behind the mountains. The hardwoods mixed in with the conifers on the hills around the pond add beautiful fall colors, especially in late afternoon light on a crisp fall day.

Directions: From the sharp right-angle turn on NY 3 in Bloomingdale, head north on 3 (East Main Street) 3.4 miles to Norman Ridge

Whiteface Mountain and the barn along Norman Ridge

Road on the right (east). Take this road a bit over 0.5 mile to both barns. Continue another mile or more past buildings and open fields until the road ends at Fletcher Farm Road. Turn right (west), then left (south) on Loop Road to go back to Bloomingdale.

To reach Moose Pond, from the sharp right-angle turn on NY 3 in Bloomingdale, head north on 3 (East Main Street) a short distance, then turn right (east) on River Road (County Route 18). It's 1.6 miles to Moose Pond Road on the right (south). Turn here, then bear right at the Y at 0.5 mile. The parking lot and trailhead are at 1.5 miles.

62. Saranac River

East of Bloomingdale, River Road follows the Saranac River, then runs along the shore of Franklin Falls Pond. There are a couple of spots along the road where the water flows right beside the road. Each of these has a slightly different vantage point and feel, and the photography here is more about the textures and details than the view. After crossing over a bay with a nice view over the pond, the road leaves the water for a bit before meeting it again by the Franklin Falls Dam. Just east of the dam, the road parallels a quiet part of the river. This is a great place to photograph shoreline detail, reflections, and perhaps some wildlife.

Directions: Heading east on River Road (County Route 18) from Bloomingdale, the road meets up with the water at 2.5 miles and again at 2.7 miles, 3.1 miles, and 3.7 miles, at a gentle bend in the river with some small rapids. There's another bend in the river only 100 feet from the road at 3.8 miles, just before the river

Detail along the Saranac River near Franklin Falls Pond

Silver Lake from the bluff at the end of the Silver Lake Bog trail

flows into Franklin Falls Pond. At 4.5 miles River Road meets up with Franklin Falls Pond and becomes Franklin Falls Road. At 4.9 miles there is a canoe access on the right (south), just before the causeway over the small bay. Some pretty views across the water to the south are accessed by a short footpath from the parking lot. The road meets the water again at 6 miles and then is back in the woods until it arrives at the bridge over the outlet at 7.3 miles. Follow Franklin Falls Road across the bridge. At about 7.5 miles is the head of Union Falls Pond, where a narrow section of still water has some beautiful reflections on a calm day, in addition to a view east across the pond before the road leaves the water once again. There are small, unpaved pullouts along the road at all of these locations.

63. Silver Lake Area

A few miles north of Wilmington and Ausable Forks are Taylor Pond, Silver Lake, Silver Lake Mountain, and the outlet of Union Falls Pond. Taylor Pond lies at the foot of rugged Catamount Mountain, which rises almost 1,800 feet above the pond's southern shore. Access to this state-owned pond is via the state campground road (day-use fee in season). There are excellent views down the pond from the head of the bay that's just to the east of the boat launch. Paddling a couple of miles on the pond brings even better views from the head of the northern bay near the center of the pond, which has wide-open views southwest down the water. There are trails around the pond as well.

The 0.9-mile trail up Silver Lake Mountain passes by several open rock ledges before reaching the south-facing view along the tree-covered summit. Views along the trail include both Taylor Pond and Silver Lake, plus the mountains surrounding them. The panoramic view from the summit ledge includes some nearby wetlands and mountains, Taylor Pond, Catamount Mountain, the Wilmington Range, and Whiteface Mountain.

The Nature Conservancy's Silver Lake Bog Preserve is an opportunity to explore and photograph some unique northern forest bogs and other habitats and wildlife. A half-mile boardwalk meanders through a black spruce–tamarack bog and northern white cedar swamp, with lots of interesting details along the way. A bit of fog creates a great mood. Beyond the boardwalk, the trail leads about another half mile through a beautiful pine forest to a rocky bluff with views of Silver Lake and Catamount and Whiteface Mountains.

Union Falls Dam on the Saranac River is just a couple of miles west of the bog, with panoramic views over the impoundment. Catamount stands tall to the south, with Esther and Whiteface farther west. Photograph from along the road right by the dam, or explore the state-owned shoreline just to the south of the dam. The southerly view can be quite nice with afternoon magic hour light on the shoreline, clouds, and mountains.

Directions: The Taylor Pond state campground entrance is on the west side of Silver Lake Road (County Route 1), 9 miles northwest of NY 9N in Ausable Forks and 8.6 miles south of NY 3 near Redford.

Parking for the trail to Silver Lake Mountain is on the east side of Silver Lake Road, 1.8 miles north of the campground. To reach the Silver Lake Bog Preserve and Union Falls Pond, continue north on Silver Lake Road and at 2.8 miles turn left (west) on Union Falls Road. In 1 mile turn left (south) on Old Hawk-eye Road to reach the trailhead at 0.5 mile on the left. Or continue on Union Falls Road to the pond access by the dam at 2.8 miles. There are unimproved campsites and access to the shoreline via an unpaved road a couple of hundred feet to the left of the dam.

64. Catamount Mountain

Just south of Taylor Pond is the rocky top of Catamount Mountain. While the rugged 1.8-mile trail starts out pretty level and rises only about 1,500 feet to the open ledges at the summit, the climbing segment of this trail is rocky and steep. In addition, there's a brief rock scramble up a short chimney on the trail near the top of the first summit. The view from the open ledges of the rocky south summit at 1.5 miles are perhaps the best from any spot along the trail, although there are a few more nice views before it reaches the actual summit. With the long ridgeline of Whiteface just to the south, and mountains across the wide-open Saranac River valley to the north, the reward for the climb is a panoramic view over the waterways and mountains of the northern Adirondacks.

Directions: From the intersection of Whiteface Veterans Memorial Highway and NY 86 in Wilmington, head west toward Whiteface. At 2.9 miles turn right (west) just before the pond by the Whiteface tollbooth on Gillespie Drive. At 6 miles turn right (north) on Roseman Lane, and at 6.8 miles turn right (east) on Plank Road/Forestdale Road. At 8.9 miles park in the wider sandy area along the north side of the road (just past the gated dirt road that cuts off to the north). The trail is on the north side of the road, just a short distance east of the parking area. There is no trail sign; look for a small opening in the trees by some red paint marks. Silver Lake Road is 5.7 miles east of the parking area via Forestdale Road and Nelson Road.

Sunrise light from the rocky summit along the trail on Catamount Mountain

Fall colors on the mountains around Catamount Mountain

Pro Tips: Since Whiteface is an isolated peak that's as much as 3,500 feet above the surrounding landscape, it makes its own weather. This causes the formation of some unique cloud formations as winds blow valley moisture over the summit, creating cloud caps, lenticular clouds, and other unique windblown cloud formations in the sky above and to the lee of the summit. A polarizer can be used to enhance the contrast between the sky and the cloud layers. A polarizer works best when used at roughly 90 degrees to the direction from which the light is coming. Ultrawide-angle focal lengths, however, are so wide that the view covers areas that are not enhanced by the polarizer, giving a quite unnatural look to the tonal changes in the sky.

Cautions: Some parts of the northern Adirondacks are rather remote, and gas stations are few and far between, with limited hours of operation. It's a good idea to fill up before heading off on these rural back roads.

Diversions: Silver Lake Road and NY 3, both east and west of their intersection, follow the Saranac River. There are numerous fishing and canoe access sites along the road, as well as views that are especially beautiful in the fall and in soft morning light. Some of the side roads along NY 3 also follow the river quite closely. Go to www.dec.ny.gov/docs/fish_marine_pdf/pfrsaranac.pdf for a map of various sections of the river in the park as well as a couple east of the park boundary.